CIVIL WAR PITTSBURGH

Forge of the Union

LEN BARCOUSKY

Charleston · London

THE
History
PRESS

Published by The History Press
Charleston, SC 29403
www.historypress.net

Front cover, top: Interior of a "sanitary steamer." *Bottom*: View of the Fort Pitt Foundry in 1862. *Images courtesy of the Senator John Heinz History Center.*
Back cover, top: Cannon making at Fort Pitt Foundry. *Courtesy of the Senator John Heinz History Center. Left*: Lincoln's visit to Pittsburgh is commemorated in a stained-glass window at the city's Smithfield Street United Church of Christ. *Courtesy Larry Roberts of the* Pittsburgh Post-Gazette.

First published 2013

Manufactured in the United States

ISBN 978.1.62619.081.8

Library of Congress CIP data applied for.

Notice: The information in this book is true and complete to the best of our knowledge. It is offered without guarantee on the part of the author or The History Press. The author and The History Press disclaim all liability in connection with the use of this book.

In memory of my father, Peter Barcousky,
a lifelong daily newspaper reader.

Contents

Foreword, by Andrew E. Masich   7

Preface: The Civil War as Breaking News   9

Acknowledgements   13

Introduction: Lincoln Salutes the Union's "Banner County"   15

1: POLITICS PRECEDES THE DRUMS OF WAR

"Wide Awakes" Rally for Lincoln   21

Republicans Win Big in Allegheny County   22

Guns of December Don't Go South   24

New President Offers an Olive Branch   27

2: AND THE WAR CAME

Stanton Warns Family of "Great Calamity"   30

A Democrat Backs Lincoln   33

Artillery Pieces from Fort Pitt Foundry Pass a Big Test   37

Pennsylvanians Show Mercy to Rebel Supporter   40

Pittsburgh Regiments Demand Better Equipment   41

3: GETTING TO KNOW THE PLAYERS

The *Gazette* Introduces Mrs. Lincoln   43

Young Abe's Unlikely Duel   45

Grant Picks Up a Nickname   47

Pittsburgh Meets a Future President   49

Life Echoes Fiction in Single Civil War Death   51

CONTENTS

4: ON THE HOMEFRONT
Both Sides Call on God's Aid at Thanksgiving   53
Confederate Sympathizer Forced to Leave   55
What War Between Brothers Really Means   56
Cooked Cat Competes for Readers' Attention   58
Allegheny Arsenal Explodes   59
Newspapers Battle over Emancipation's Meaning   62
Friendly Gunfire Greets Lincoln's Proclamation   65
Allegheny Boys Don't Lack Ways to Find Trouble   67
City Digs in as Lee Invades the North   69
Pittsburgh's Sanitary Fair Proves Better Than Average   74
Real Math Trumps Democrats' Optimism   77

5: NEWS FROM THE BATTLEFIELD
Reunion at Fortress Monroe   82
Pittsburgh's Negley Tries Tough Love in Tennessee   84
Revenge for Bull Run at South Mountain   86
Pittsburgh Rifles in the Front Lines at Antietam   88
Union Pays for Delay at Fredericksburg   90
A POW Tours the South   93
Pittsburgh Ships Offer Refuge to All Union Wounded   97
Rebels Don "Sunday Clothing" for Chambersburg Raid   99
"Wilderness" Bullet Ends Life of General Hays   101

6: THE GAZETTE COVERS THE CAPITAL
War Wakes Up Washington   105
A Pennsylvanian Faces Russian Exile   108
Emancipation Arrives Early   110
Pittsburgher's Visit to Jeff Davis Proves a Hoax   112

7: AS THE GUNS FALL SILENT
Pittsburgh Mourns Lincoln's Death   114
Andrew Johnson Faces a Tough Crowd   117
Grand Army of the Republic Veterans March in Final Muster   119
GAR Postscript   121

Bibliography and Further Reading   123
Index   125
About the Author   128

Foreword

Remembering Pittsburgh's Civil War

The period from 2011 to 2015 marks the 150th anniversary of the Civil War. All across America, the sesquicentennial will be remembered with parades and reenactments, films and television specials, YouTube videos and blogs. Chroniclers of the past have, in fact, authored more books and articles on the Civil War than any other event in history until, it seemed, that nothing more could be written. Yet this singular event shaped our nation and the people we have become. The stories warrant retelling as they are replete with lessons both sobering and inspiring. They are of ordinary people—men and women, black and white, soldier and civilian—living in extraordinary times.

Pittsburgh Post-Gazette reporter Len Barcousky has found a way to bring these stories to life by presenting them just as Americans perceived them, through the pages of their daily newspaper. Barcousky has a newsman's eye for a good story well told and has combed the archives to rediscover the news of tragedy, heroism, love and humor. The reader will be reminded that there is a contingency in history—nothing is inevitable—and chance can determine different paths in our lives. The future was not foretold for the people of the past. Imagine as you read *Civil War Pittsburgh* that the outcome of the struggle is still in doubt—just as it was for the readers 150 years ago.

The Civil War touched all Americans in some way. Pittsburgh men and women contributed significantly to the rising public awareness of the horror of slavery and the growing abolition movement. Allegheny County played a role in electing the first Republican president in the election of 1860 that triggered the secession of the Southern states and the establishment of the Confederacy. Pittsburghers prevented cannons and war ordnance from being shipped to the rebellious South. War-related industry boomed, and Pittsburgh's mills and factories became the "arsenal of the Union." Smoking foundries and forges worked day and night, turning out the largest iron cannons ever cast—innovations that other world powers could not duplicate. Female workers replaced men at Allegheny Arsenal and suffered and died in the worst industrial accident of the war when the ammunition laboratories ignited and the subsequent blasts rocked the city. Though the fighting never reached the confluence of the three rivers, it came perilously close, and the threat of attack and sabotage was real enough that factory workers and citizens excavated massive fortifications on the high ground surrounding the city.

The Pittsburgh Sanitary Commission fair raised funds for wounded soldiers and men serving in the field while many women and girls knitted socks, rolled bandages and provided necessary supplies for men at the front. Pittsburgh's sons sprang to the call to arms, serving on land and sea in numbers that far exceeded those of other regions and states. Most western Pennsylvanians lost family, friends or acquaintances. As battles raged in the South and closer to home during Lee's 1863 invasion of Pennsylvania, eager readers and anxious families pored over the news reports and lists of the dead and wounded.

Though Abraham Lincoln never again returned to Pittsburgh after his inaugural train steamed from the city en route to Washington in February 1861, he returned to Pennsylvania in November 1863 to dedicate a national cemetery—the first of its kind—for the nearly eight thousand soldiers slain at Gettysburg, the greatest battle of the war. It was here that the president spoke the words that helped the people of the state and nation find meaning in a war that had become more terrible than any would have imagined in the early days of the conflict. He believed that the dead of Gettysburg had died not in vain but rather for a "new birth of freedom" for that nation "of the people, by the people, for the people." It is altogether fitting that we should remember the Civil War and resolve to build the nation that those who have gone before had so nobly begun.

ANDREW E. MASICH
President and CEO of the Senator John Heinz History Center in Pittsburgh

Preface

The Civil War as Breaking News

Novelist William Faulkner famously wrote, "The past is never dead. It's not even past." That's certainly true when it comes to the Civil War, a subject that remains strongly connected to the present as our nation marks the sesquicentennial of the conflict. After 150 years, people still can't even agree on what to call it. Options include "The War Between the States," "The Southern Insurrection," "The Lost Cause" and even "The War of Northern Aggression."

Here in Pittsburgh, we're still reexamining the whys and wherefores of our own Civil War–linked events. Among the better known is the Allegheny Arsenal explosion. That disaster, which killed seventy-eight people in September 1863, was recently the subject for a "cold case" coroner's jury.

The proximate cause was loose gunpowder, most likely ignited by a spark from an iron wagon wheel or a horseshoe. But responsibility for unsafe conditions at the facility rested with the U.S. Army officers who supervised the facility, the modern coroner's jurors decided.

The two-and-a-half-hour mock inquest drew a standing-room-only crowd to Pittsburgh's Senator John Heinz History Center to hear testimony from a half dozen experts who were familiar with the tragedy. The victims, mostly young women and girls, had been assembling cartridges in workrooms at the arsenal, located in what was then the Pittsburgh suburb of Lawrenceville.

Civil War Pittsburgh is based almost solely on contemporary reports that appeared in local newspapers, primarily the *Daily Pittsburgh Gazette* and the

Allegheny Arsenal, in Pittsburgh's Lawrenceville neighborhood, was the site of the worst civilian disaster of the Civil War. Photo shows the main gate in about 1900. *Courtesy Senator John Heinz History Center.*

Pittsburgh Post, during the conflict. These stories reveal what local residents read and knew and how they reacted to events like the arsenal explosion, the Battle of Gettysburg and the assassination of Abraham Lincoln.

Some stories, like the disaster at the arsenal, are generally remembered, even if many of the details have grown foggy. Others, like the efforts of residents in December 1860 to halt the shipment of heavy arms from Pittsburgh to what would soon become the Confederacy, are less well known. A few, like a first-person report by a Union prisoner of war describing what he saw on a two-thousand-mile railroad journey through the South, have been forgotten for a century and a half.

Pennsylvania sits on the Mason-Dixon line, the traditional border between the North and South. When the war began, the South, in the form of what was then the Virginia Panhandle, began just thirty-five miles from where the Monongahela and Allegheny Rivers merged to form the Ohio River. The result was that while the majority of Pittsburgh and Allegheny County residents were supporters of the Union and Lincoln, the area had its share of people with Southern sympathies.

Libby Prison, a former tobacco warehouse in Richmond, Virginia, where Josiah Copley was kept as a prisoner of war. *Courtesy Senator John Heinz History Center.*

The city's major newspapers demonstrated that split. The *Gazette* was strongly Republican and backed Lincoln and emancipation while the *Pittsburgh Post* backed the Democrats and states' rights.

Pennsylvania's farms and factories were always a tempting target for Southern armies seeking supplies. An invasion of the state would also bring the war home to the North. In the summer of 1863, after Confederate general Robert E. Lee crossed the Potomac River, Abraham Lincoln met at the White House with a visitor from Pittsburgh. The industrial city at the Forks of the Ohio was a more attractive target for the Rebel army than Harrisburg, Lincoln warned him.

Pittsburgh residents recognized the danger. By the end of June, as many as 6,800 factory workers, miners and store clerks, including some of the city's black residents, were digging entrenchments to repel possible attacks from General J.E.B. Stuart's fast-moving cavalry. During those anxious weeks, the Civil War was the top local story in Pittsburgh.

Time spent going through microfilm copies of the newspapers can turn up unlikely relationships. Josiah Copley Jr. was captured at the Battle of

Stones River, Tennessee, on the last day of 1862. The son of a Pittsburgh newspaper editor, he wrote about his experiences for the *Gazette* after he was released in a prisoner exchange.

His sister, Mary Copley, married transportation mogul William Thaw Sr. shortly after the end of the Civil War. Thaw assembled one of the nation's largest fortunes through investments in canals, steamboats and railroads.

Despite their later record of philanthropy, the senior Thaws are best remembered because their son, Harry Kendall Thaw, shot and killed architect Stanford White in 1906 at Madison Square Garden in New York. Newspapers called the subsequent legal proceedings "The Trial of the Century." Harry Thaw, who believed that White had had an affair with his chorus-girl wife, was ultimately acquitted on grounds of insanity and sent to a mental institution.

The danger in looking at microfilm copies is getting caught up pursuing unrelated issues—like the link between Harry Thaw and his Uncle Josiah. But browsing can also turn up an occasional gem involving one of the most famous figures in American history.

Abraham Lincoln was known as someone who had a joke for any occasion. On June 18, 1863, he met in the White House with an anonymous Pittsburgh resident who wanted to set up a mission to serve newly emancipated slaves, referred to as Freedmen.

According to a letter from Washington that the Pittsburgh correspondent wrote to the *Gazette*, published on June 22, the busy president was meeting simultaneously with a delegation of visitors from Connecticut. The events described in the letter took place three days after Lincoln had issued a call for the states to provide another 100,000 militia troops.

"Why, we have been calling out the militia lately, and there are as many here from Connecticut as would nearly make a company," the president told the group from the Nutmeg State. His Pittsburgh visitor wrote that Lincoln was hinting that his Connecticut callers should be in uniform. Perhaps, the president mused aloud, they still believed the war would be over soon: "[As] the man said to Noah, when he refused to give him a passage in the ark—'It is not going to be much of a shower after all.'"

The "shower" lasted almost two more years, and the cost in blood and treasure was heavy. The Pittsburgh stories on the following pages provide glimpses, via next-day news reports, into what life was like in southwestern Pennsylvania during that history-making time.

Acknowledgements

From the earliest days of the *Pittsburgh Gazette* in 1786, its editors and reporters have understood how the past can mold the present and the future. That understanding is reflected in the time and space the *Pittsburgh Post-Gazette* continues to devote to stories about the history of this region. I am grateful for the support of the top editors of this newspaper, especially publisher and editor-in-chief John Robinson Block and executive editor David M. Shribman. My immediate supervisors, including Tom Birdsong, Ed Blazina and Virginia Kopas Joe, have given me the time to work on these stories as part of the newspaper's 150th anniversary commemoration of the Civil War. Thanks also to Gary Rotstein, the editor of the *Post-Gazette*'s page-two features, where versions of many of these stories first appeared.

I appreciate the excellent work of the newspaper's copy desk, headed by David Garth. They regularly save me from myself through their questions, challenges and suggestions for improvement. *Post-Gazette* photography is an important part of this book. I remain in special debt to Andy Starnes, Larry Roberts and Jim Mendenhall for their cooperation in assembling photos and engravings. Allison Latcheran, the newspaper's marketing services manager, supported this project and worked out the terms that turned these columns into a book.

Writing Pittsburgh history would be impossible without the help of local libraries and their skilled librarians. Their ranks include Angelika Kane and Steve Karlinchak at the *Post-Gazette* and chief librarian Art Louderback, former chief archivist David Grinnell and current chief archivist Matthew

Strauss at the Senator John Heinz History Center. Reference staff members in the Pennsylvania Room of the Carnegie Library of Pittsburgh have been helpful, pleasant and patient on my many trips to that institution.

My wife, Barbara, once again has patiently listened to me talk out this project. She never failed to ask about what new snippets of local history I had unearthed during my expeditions to the Carnegie Library.

Newspaper stories are ephemeral by nature. Readers want to know what is happening now. I have found, however, that every old edition of the *Post-Gazette*, and many of the region's other newspapers, contains something worth reprinting. The following notice to journalists was first printed 152 years ago, but its advice remains valid. On March 6, 1861, the editors of the *Pittsburgh Dispatch* informed those who sought to be published: "CORRESPONDENTS should study brevity more carefully. We gladly give place to news of incidents from any quarters, but our columns are so crowded that we cannot find room for mere words."

Introduction

Lincoln Salutes the Union's "Banner County"

Abraham Lincoln was one of two American presidents-elect on the way to their inaugurations when he visited Pittsburgh on Valentine's Day 1861.

Lincoln's train had been scheduled to pull into the station in Allegheny City, now Pittsburgh's North Side, at 5:20 p.m. It arrived instead in heavy rain and darkness, almost three hours late. He had been delayed by a freight-train derailment that blocked the line between Baden and Rochester, the *Daily Pittsburgh Gazette* reported the next morning.

That same day's paper carried a story with an Alabama dateline. "Hon. Jefferson Davis will leave Jackson, Miss., tonight for Montgomery," the story began. Davis, a West Point graduate and former U.S. secretary of war and senator from Mississippi, had been elected provisional president of the Confederate States of America. With major stops planned in Chattanooga, Tennessee, and Atlanta, Georgia, he was heading for Montgomery, the new capital of the breakaway Southern states.

While Pittsburgh and Allegheny County voters had strongly backed Republicans in recent gubernatorial and presidential races, the region had plenty of Democrats who were in sympathy with the Southern cause. The newspapers reflected in their coverage of Lincoln's overnight visit the region's political differences. While the *Gazette* supported the GOP, the *Pittsburgh Post* was the voice of the region's Democrats.

Both papers agreed that the area around the Federal Street station had been crowded at 5:00 p.m., shortly before Lincoln's train was due to arrive.

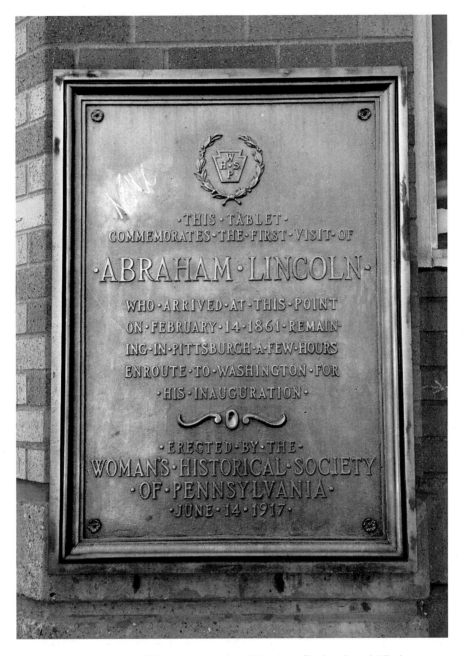

A bronze plaque notes the 1861 visit by Abraham Lincoln to Pittsburgh and Allegheny City, which is now the North Side. The memorial is at Federal Street and South Commons. *Courtesy Robin Rombach of the* Pittsburgh Post-Gazette.

The *Post* reported the next morning that a driving rain and too long a wait had sent most spectators home, leaving Federal Street almost deserted.

Though he agreed that many people had gone, the *Gazette*'s reporter wrote that "thousands, however, remained about the depot and under the platforms" when Lincoln's train arrived. The reporter continued his description: "His appearance set the people wild with excitement, and cries of 'speech, speech' intermingled with continuous cheering, indicated that they were not to be put off without a word or two." Standing up in the carriage that was to take him across an Allegheny River bridge into Pittsburgh, Lincoln complied, but he didn't say much. "He alluded to the delay of the train and the inauspiciousness of the weather," according to the newspaper. He promised to speak at length the next morning.

Lincoln was to spend the night at Pittsburgh's finest hotel, the Monongahela House on Smithfield Street. "So dense was the gathering [in front of the hotel entrance], that the military had to clear a passage with their bayonets, when the President-elect stepped from the carriage and entered the hotel." The crowd wanted more. It was from the balcony of the hotel that Lincoln, a consummate politician, made his often quoted remark about the region. No words of praise were necessary about Allegheny County, he said, "as it was already widely known as the 'banner county' of the State, if not of the whole Union."

The Monongahela House was demolished in 1935, but the bed that Lincoln is believed to have slept in survives. It was recently reassembled and put on display at the Senator John Heinz History Center.

Lincoln, although he was president-elect, spent his brief time in Pittsburgh behaving like a candidate still running for office. He made three short speeches and a major address. He shook hands, tipped his hat to crowds of well-wishers and met with political supporters and elected officials from the county, Pittsburgh and Allegheny City.

And if a memoir of a North Side woman is accurate, he kissed at least one pretty girl.

Susan Cooper Walker was born on Wylie Avenue in April 1852 but soon moved with her family to Brighton Road. When Lincoln came to Pittsburgh, "we were taken to the railroad station to see him," she wrote in a 1943 memoir called *When I Look Back and Think*. The book, dictated more than eighty years after the events it describes, does not make clear if the Cooper children went out to see Lincoln arrive or leave. "With us went Mary Morrison, an older cousin," Walker recalled. "She was lovely to look at. When he saw her, Abraham Lincoln said, 'You're a pretty girl,' and kissed

A 1935 photograph shows Allegheny County carpenters carrying what is believed to be the bed that Lincoln slept in while on a visit to Pittsburgh. *Courtesy the* Pittsburgh Post-Gazette.

Monongahela House in the early twentieth century. Lincoln spoke from the balcony at right in February 1861. *Courtesy Senator John Heinz History Center.*

her." Initially indignant, Mary Morrison "lived to brag about that kiss," her cousin wrote.

When I Look Back and Think and an 1861 daily diary kept by Daisy Davis Wilson are in the archives of the Heinz History Center. The mother of twin babies, Daisy Davis Wilson was in her early twenties when Lincoln visited. "Worked as hard as I could all morning," she wrote on February 14. "Then Thompson, Ma, Mr. W. and I went to the station to see President's train pass." Perhaps commenting on the dreary weather, she noted being "very uncomfortable." Mr. W. was her husband, Samuel Jennings Wilson, a Presbyterian minister and a teacher at what was then called Western Theological Seminary.

Lincoln's bad luck with weather continued the next morning. A "smart rain" was falling on February 15 as he prepared to speak once again from the balcony of the Monongahela House, the *Post* reported. Whatever the political leanings of its editor and on-the-scene reporter, James P. Barr, the *Post* did not underplay the enthusiasm for Lincoln that morning. "The street in front of the Monongahela House was literally covered with citizens anxious to see and hear the President-elect," the paper reported on February 16. Inside the hotel, the crowd was "so thickly populated…that it was almost impossible to remove from place to place."

Pittsburgh mayor George Wilson introduced Lincoln not only as "the chief magistrate of our nation but also as the harbinger of peace to our distracted country." Even as the country was splitting apart, Lincoln's tone was conciliatory. Despite secession votes in several Southern states, he told the crowd he believed regional differences would be worked out. "[T]here is no crisis, excepting such a one as may be gotten up at any time by turbulent men, aided by designing politicians," he said. Knowing his audience, Lincoln also pledged continued support for tariffs on manufactured goods, a position that would have endeared him to Pittsburgh's business community.

He spoke for about thirty minutes. The size of the crowd almost made him late getting back across the Allegheny River to the train that was to take him to Cleveland, his next major stop. General James S. Negley, who was in charge of security, appealed to the crowd at the railroad station to step back, and Lincoln's party passed "one by one in Indian file" to the train platform. "The impression which [Lincoln] made upon our citizens generally, by his personal bearing and public remarks, was highly favorable," the *Gazette*'s editor wrote. Summing up the visit in the *Post*, editor Barr would offer only a half-hearted compliment: "Mr. Lincoln [is not] as ungainly in personal appearance, nor as ugly in the face as he has been represented," he wrote on February 17. The description continues, "He is by no means a handsome man, [but] his facial angles would not break a looking glass."

Despite Lincoln's confident words in Pittsburgh, the secession crisis worsened. Three days after Lincoln left the city, Jefferson Davis took the oath of office as Confederate president. Lincoln was not inaugurated until two weeks later. Once he became president, Lincoln refused a demand from the Confederate government that he withdraw Union forces from Fort Sumter, which controlled the entrance to South Carolina's Charleston Harbor. The Confederates launched an artillery barrage on April 12, 1861, forcing the fort's surrender and beginning the four-year conflict.

Chapter 1

Politics Precedes the Drums of War

"Wide Awakes" Rally for Lincoln

Politics may have played as large a role as mathematics in estimating crowd size for the "Grand Republican Mass Meeting at Pittsburgh" on September 26, 1860.

"Five Thousand Live Republicans" took part in a torch-lit procession, according to the next morning's edition of the *Daily Pittsburgh Gazette*. The marchers were part of a GOP-affiliated organization called the "Wide Awakes." The quasi-military marching society provided security at Republican events.

The solidly Republican newspaper estimated that 100,000 people gathered the next day to watch and participate in a rally and election parade that wound its way through downtown Pittsburgh and Allegheny City, now the North Side. "The Great Republican Demonstration of yesterday exceeded in magnitude any political gathering that has ever taken place in this section of the State, and we doubt whether it has been surpassed in any other part of the Union," the *Gazette* said on September 28.

The *Pittsburgh Post*, an unabashedly Democratic newspaper, scoffed at the numbers. It rejected the *Gazette's* estimate of 100,000 spectators and participants out of hand, noting that number was nearly equal to the total population of Allegheny County. In its September 29 edition, the *Post* reported that the GOP's daylight procession included exactly 222 carriages and wagons, 1,027 horses and 2,052 marchers. The newspaper offered no estimate on the number of watchers.

Whatever the actual number of participants and spectators, the Pittsburgh rallies, in support of the presidential candidacy of Abraham Lincoln, were big events and indications of the passions aroused by the 1860 election. "Our city last night was in a blaze of light, from thousands of torches borne by a great army of gallant and true-hearted Republican Wide Awakes," the *Gazette* said. Their tramp down what is now Liberty Avenue "was conducted with military precision…and the best of order prevailed through the long march."

"The windows and doorways of a large number of the houses along the route…were filled with ladies, who literally showered down floral wreaths and bouquets on the moving throng below them," continued the paper. This being Pittsburgh, "there was a very handsome display of fireworks." The combination of pyrotechnics, lit torches and the Wide Awakes "going through their various maneuvers made a very imposing appearance."

The next day's activities included a second parade and ended with a rally in what is now West Park on Pittsburgh's North Side. Orators included Ohio senator Benjamin Wade, former Ohio governor Tom Corwin, Pennsylvania representative John Covode and GOP candidate for governor Andrew Curtin. The speakers were so numerous and the crowds so large that four separate podiums were set up. Still, according to the *Gazette*, "tens of thousands on the ground…could not get near the speakers" and missed out on the campaign rhetoric.

In its coverage, the *Post* was unimpressed. It compared the event to "the ancient 'Feast of Fools,'" describing it as a "farce." It also warned Pittsburgh business owners that their ironworks, glass factories and textile mills might face economic retribution from Southern buyers for their support of Lincoln and the Republicans.

REPUBLICANS WIN BIG IN ALLEGHENY COUNTY

The year 1860, like the year 2010, was a good one for Republicans in Pennsylvania.

On October 9, the party's candidate for governor, Andrew Curtin, beat Democratic hopeful Henry Donnel Foster. Curtin's win was thought to be a good omen for the upcoming presidential contest on November 6.

Pittsburgh's Democrats, however, were not ready to give up the fight. "Let no Democrat neglect to cast his VOTE TO-DAY," the *Pittsburgh Post* urged on the morning of the election. "Up and at them, Boys!" The newspaper's coverage included the list of presidential electors who were pledged to support Northern Democratic candidate Stephen Douglas in his contest against Republican Abraham Lincoln. Two other candidates were also in the race: Southern Democrat John Breckenridge and Constitutional-Union hopeful John Bell. Turnout would be important, and the *Post* advised voters not to be disheartened by the party's defeat in the governor's race: "Empires are not lost by single battles, and we have a great Democratic empire to regain. It will be an act of cowardice to stay away from the polls now."

The newspaper was not pleased with the outcome. Lincoln was elected with strong support from Northern voters but lost the Southern and Border States. In Allegheny County, Republicans had built up momentum. Lincoln's vote totals in November were higher than those received by GOP gubernatorial candidate Curtin a month earlier. While Lincoln had a clear victory in the electoral votes, which are distributed winner-take-all style in each state, he did not get a majority of all votes cast. His win was "a triumph of sectionalism," the *Post* concluded on November 7.

"The Democracy [Democratic Party], since the result of the State election, have been disheartened and discouraged," according to the *Post*. "They have not worked with their accustomed energy…a great and useful party, through its own folly and divisions has suffered itself to be temporarily overthrown by its enemies." While talk of secession already was widespread in the Southern states, the *Post* urged caution and loyalty. "Let us all hope for the best, and as Democrats and true men, stand by the Constitution and Union at all hazards."

In an 1858 speech, just after he had been nominated to run for the U.S. Senate from Illinois, Lincoln had warned that over time the nation could not continue half slave and half free. "A house divided against itself cannot stand," he said. The *Post* echoed his remark the day after the election: "The house of the Democracy has been divided against itself and it could not stand."

The city's Republicans, on the other hand, were jubilant. When returns from Philadelphia and New York came in showing big majorities for Lincoln, "a scene followed which baffled all description." The *Daily Pittsburgh Gazette* reported: "Round after round of the most deafening cheers were given; hats were waved and some thrown into the air; there was clapping and stamping and every demonstration that could be employed to express the wild and uncontrollable enthusiasms that pervaded the tremendous assemblage."

GUNS OF DECEMBER DON'T GO SOUTH

Christmas 1860 was one of the most anxious times in the history of the United States. Following the election of Abraham Lincoln on November 6, secessionists throughout the South, led by the actions of citizens of South Carolina, had begun organizing conventions to vote on withdrawal from the Union.

President James Buchanan, who believed that secession was illegal but that there was nothing he could do to stop it, appeared paralyzed. Still, he would remain president and continue to set national policy for the next two critical months.

The *Daily Pittsburgh Gazette*, which had strongly supported Lincoln's candidacy, had long given up on Buchanan, the only native-born Pennsylvanian to be elected president. When the president called for a

JAMES BUCHANAN.

JOHN B. FLOYD.

Above, left: President James Buchanan eventually countermanded the order to ship cannons south. Image from *Harper's Pictorial History of the Civil War Part First. Courtesy Senator John Heinz History Center.*

Above, right: U.S. secretary of war John B. Floyd, who ordered heavy arms shipped south, later became a Confederate general. Image from *Harper's Pictorial History of the Civil War Part First. Courtesy Senator John Heinz History Center.*

national day of fasting and prayer, Russell Errett, the editor of the *Gazette*, wrote that the country's "great sin against Heaven [had been] in electing JAMES BUCHANAN to the Presidency." His administration "had been a crime from the beginning to the end," Errett wrote on December 18. Its "weakness, vacillation and temporizing policy" had emboldened traitors "in five or six Southern states" who threatened to break up the Union. Errett continued, "[I]nstead of invoking the arm of the law to punish their treason, he invokes us to come up before God…confess our sins in voting for LINCOLN, and pray for divine help to enable us to conquer the stubborn convictions of our heart."

By mid-December, talk of secession had advanced beyond words with Federal garrisons outside Charleston, South Carolina, under virtual siege. The state's governor had warned President Buchanan not to make any efforts to resupply or reinforce with more troops Forts Moultrie and Sumter. Major Robert Anderson commanded the garrisons. The *Gazette* reported that his wife had visited Buchanan "a few days ago and remonstrated that he had placed her husband where he must be murdered or degraded."

The newspaper also printed what it said was a letter from John B. Floyd, a former governor of Virginia who was Buchanan's secretary of war. In the letter, he promised out-going South Carolina governor William Henry Gist that no more Federal troops would be sent to the forts outside Charleston. "I will resign before it shall be done," Floyd wrote, according to the newspaper.

Even as Southern states made plans to leave the Union, regular supplies of arms and ammunition continued to be shipped below the Mason-Dixon line. That issue exploded on Christmas Day. "Evidence of Treason of the National Government" was the headline on the *Gazette*'s story that morning. "The heart of the people was stirred to the utmost indignation, yesterday, upon learning that Secretary FLOYD…ordered most of the cannons at the U.S. Arsenal, here, to the extent of 100 or more, to be shipped to New Orleans and Galveston."

"The people could hardly believe so astounding a story, at first," the newspaper said. "[B]ut every inquiry only confirmed the report. There is the utmost activity at the arsenal; and the steamboat *SILVER WAVE*, we learn, has been chartered to convey the guns from hence to their southern destination." Once the guns were transported below the Mason-Dixon line, they likely would be captured by secessionist Southerners and turned against the Federal government.

In the 1860s, newspaper type had to be set one character at a time. When late-breaking information arrived close to deadline, it had to be squeezed

Bronze plaque mounted on the front of the Allegheny County Courthouse describes the 1860 public meeting that ultimately delayed the shipment of war materials to what became the Confederacy. *Courtesy Robin Rombach of the* Pittsburgh Post-Gazette.

in wherever it would fit. The *Gazette*'s December 25 edition contained a postscript updating the artillery shipment story. A total of 124 guns—not 100—were to be moved, the newspaper reported. It said 78 were headed to Galveston, Texas, and 46 to Ship Island, Mississippi. News reporting shifted over into advocacy with a call to action in the last paragraph of the story. "Let the people assemble today, or tomorrow, and utter their emphatic No! to the order of the Secretary of War," the newspaper urged.

Secretary of War Floyd might have believed most Pittsburgh residents would be too involved in Christmas preparations to pay attention to the news. He was wrong. In response, Pittsburgh residents held two mass meetings to protest the decision by the lame-duck Buchanan administration to ship the weapons.

Opponents, however, were in a ticklish spot. Buchanan remained the duly elected president for two more months. Any violent protests to stop the shipments could be seen as mirror images of the kind of actions that many Southerners were taking to break up the Union. Following a Christmas Day meeting in the office of Pittsburgh mayor George Wilson, the city leaders sent a telegram to Buchanan imploring him to reverse the shipment order, the *Gazette* reported on December 27. A second public meeting followed that same day at the county courthouse. "[T]he sidewalks on Fifth street [now Fifth Avenue], leading to the Court House were thronged with masses of people going to the meeting," the newspaper reported the next day. So many people attended that the session had to be moved outside. Pittsburgh congressman James K. Moorhead warned that South Carolina politicians, who had voted on December 20 for their state to leave the Union, were hoping for violence in Pittsburgh. "[N]othing resembling an overt act of treason should be committed," he said. If the president could not be persuaded to rescind Floyd's order, "let the guns go."

Preparations to ship the guns moved slowly, and the *Gazette* hoped, on December 31, that cold weather would come to the aid of the Union. "Perhaps Jack Frost will turn patriot in this extremity and lay an embargo on the navigation of the Ohio," the *Gazette* speculated.

Secretary Floyd had threatened to resign if Buchanan took a harder line against the South, and on December 29, he carried out his threat. After several more days of dithering, Buchanan and his divided cabinet agreed to hold onto the artillery. "The order is revoked," Congressman Moorhead wrote to Mayor Wilson on January 3. "The guns don't go."

Former Pittsburgh lawyer Edwin M. Stanton, who had just been named Buchanan's last attorney general, confirmed the decision. "Floyd's order respecting the shipment of arms has been countermanded," he wrote to Wilson on the same day. "No little excitement was created in the city yesterday upon the reception of the news that Secretary Floyd's order for the removal of the guns from the Arsenal here to points in the South, had been countermanded," the *Gazette* reported on January 4. "Our citizens have accomplished, in a peaceable way, all they desired and it is to be hoped that the 'big guns' will not again be disturbed until there is a more urgent necessity for their removal."

NEW PRESIDENT OFFERS AN OLIVE BRANCH

Thanks to the communications revolution brought about by the telegraph, Pittsburgh readers could debate the meaning of Abraham Lincoln's inaugural address within hours of the time it was delivered in Washington, D.C.

Lincoln took his oath of office on March 4, 1861, and Pittsburgh's daily newspapers put out "extras" that same afternoon and evening. Journalism is always the art of the possible, and those earliest editions, hurried into print, contained garbled phrases and missing words.

Abraham Lincoln, in image from *Harper's Pictorial History of the Civil War Part First,* called on "better angels of our nature" in his first inaugural address. *Courtesy Senator John Heinz History Center.*

The next morning, the *Daily Pittsburgh Gazette* apologized to its readers for the errors, "which in many instances destroyed the meaning of whole sentences."

"We this morning give a more correct copy of this interesting document," the paper said on March 5. "When the reader is informed that this address was sent out over the wires and put in type in less than two hours from the time of its delivery in Washington, they will readily excuse the printers and the telegraph operators for the errors."

The *Gazette* hailed Lincoln's speech for its firm but not radical tone. "It will be observed that Mr. Lincoln does not recognize the abominable doctrine of secession, but has announced his determination to administer the laws according to the requirements of his oath," the paper noted with approval.

"There is no bravado, no irritating threats…and yet no language could more distinctly and emphatically declare his purpose, faithfully to execute the laws and maintain the Union in its integrity."

Not surprisingly, the *Pittsburgh Post* was scornful of the new president's remarks. Its editor appeared equally upset about "the enormous price of sixty dollars" that the Associated Press news service charged for its special dispatch of the address. That $60 translates to between $1,200 and $1,500 in modern currency. Lincoln's speech "from which so much was expected…was, we venture to say, a sad disappointment," the *Post* opined on March 6. The olive branch that Lincoln seemed to extend toward the South—a promise that he would not interfere with slavery where it now existed—was meaningless, according to the *Post*, because the Constitution already legalized slavery.

The two real issues were whether the Republicans would bend enough to allow slavery into new territories and whether Lincoln would seek to retake Federal property held by secessionist governments. "We are grieved to look over this production of Mr. Lincoln's and to think that so puerile a paper should have come to dash down the hopes and sadden the hearts of the people," the paper concluded.

History generally has favored the *Gazette*'s more generous analysis of the speech's tone and content.

Both papers included the full text of Lincoln's address, including its often-quoted conclusion.

"I am loath to close," the president said in the version printed by the *Gazette* on March 5. The paper continued the extract:

> *We are not enemies, but friends. We must not be enemies.*
>
> *Though passion may have strained, it must not break our bonds of affection. The mystic chords of memory stretching from every battle field and patriot grave, to every loving heart and hearthstone, all over this broad land, will yet swell the chorus of the Union, when again touched, as surely they will be, by the better angels of our nature.*

Chapter 2

And the War Came

STANTON WARNS FAMILY OF "GREAT CALAMITY"

While lawyers are encouraged to anticipate the worst that can happen, U.S. attorney general Edwin M. Stanton in January 1861 was optimistic about a peaceful resolution of differences between Northern and Southern states.

"I have never doubted that we should in the end pass safely through the present troubles," he wrote to his brother-in-law, James Adam Hutchison Jr., in a letter dated January 15, 1861. Stanton's letter to Hutchison, a Pittsburgh lawyer, is in a collection of family correspondence and photographs in the archives at the Senator John Heinz History Center. That correspondence offers a glimpse into the life and thinking of a man who would become a member of Abraham Lincoln's Cabinet and one of his closest advisers during the Civil War.

Stanton, who grew up in Steubenville, Ohio, attended Kenyon College, studied law and began his professional career in his native state. In 1847, he relocated to the booming industrial city of Pittsburgh. His first wife, Mary, had died in 1841 while he was still building his Ohio law practice. Following a two-year courtship, he married Ellen Hutchison in 1856. Sixteen years younger than her new husband, she came from a wealthy and socially prominent Pittsburgh family. After Stanton and his family moved to Washington, D.C., he maintained close ties to his wife's Pittsburgh relatives, keeping in touch via letters to various family members.

Edwin M. Stanton, Lincoln's secretary of war, practiced law in Pittsburgh for several years before relocating to Washington. Image is from *Harper's Pictorial History of the Civil War Part First. Courtesy Senator John Heinz History Center.*

Terry H. Wells, of Evanston, Illinois, a descendant of the Hutchison family, donated the material dealing with Stanton and the Hutchison family to the history center in 2001. While James Adam Hutchison moved to Chicago after the Civil War, family members maintained their links to Allegheny County. Many are buried in Pittsburgh's Homewood Cemetery. The Hutchison materials include several photographs of Stanton, some made in the studio of photographer Mathew Brady, who became famous for his Civil War pictures. Another image is of a marble bust of Stanton that was created for a monument to him in Steubenville.

The nineteen Stanton letters represent what David Grinnell, formerly the chief archivist at the history center, calls "just a sliver" of the archive's holdings on Pittsburgh's prominent, and intermarried, Hutchison, Dallas, Wells and Wilkins families.

Stanton usually wrote in a firm hand, using dark ink on fine paper that has deteriorated little in the past century and a half. It is, nevertheless, occasionally difficult to make out some of his words.

An antislavery Democrat, Stanton became U.S. attorney general during the final months of the disastrous administration of President James Buchanan. While sympathetic to the South and its "Peculiar Institution," as slavery was sometimes called, Buchanan believed that secession was illegal. Unfortunately, he also believed there was nothing he could do as president to stop states from breaking up the Union. Many historians credit Stanton with stiffening Buchanan's spine during the period between the election of Lincoln in November 1860 and his inauguration the following March.

As Stanton joined Buchanan's cabinet in December 1860, Southern Democrats were leaving it, as were members of the House and Senate from states preparing to secede. Those departing included Secretary of War John B. Floyd, a Virginian. Floyd had been at the center of the dispute over the shipment of artillery from Pittsburgh to forts in the South. In the face of noisy protests in Pittsburgh, Buchanan ultimately reversed Floyd's order to send weapons to soon-to-be secessionists.

By January 15, when Stanton wrote from Washington to his brother-in-law, four Southern states had left the Union: South Carolina, Mississippi, Florida and Alabama. Still, he remained hopeful that the worst was over and that secession fever would break. "In respect to political affairs, there has been no material change for the last two or three days," he wrote to Hutchison. "The Separatists are all out of the cabinet now and we are united, I think, in resolution to do all in our power to uphold the government."

"The government cannot be overthrown except by treason and even that could only succeed for a short time," he wrote, underlining the word "cannot."

"I think the Southern riots will soon exhaust themselves, and that before the 4th of March peace will be restored and business re-established with more activity than ever," he concluded. March 4 was the date of Lincoln's inauguration.

On February 11, Lincoln left Springfield, Illinois, on a circuitous pre-inaugural train trip that would take him to Washington. His stops included Pittsburgh, where he avoided discussing the issue of slavery, saying only that he expected cooler heads would prevail. They did not. Jefferson Davis was inaugurated as Confederate president on February 18, two weeks before Lincoln took his oath of office. Three more states— Georgia, Louisiana and Texas—had voted to leave the Union by the time Lincoln was sworn in.

After he became president, Lincoln reiterated his promise not to interfere with slavery where it existed. But he also expressed his determination to maintain Federal control over Southern military installations, including Fort Sumter, located at the entrance to the harbor at Charleston, South Carolina.

Shortly after Lincoln informed South Carolina's secessionist governor that he planned to resupply the garrison, Confederate artillery fired on the fort. It was the early morning of April 12. Its outgunned commander, Robert Anderson, surrendered the next day to the Rebels.

Stanton, out of government following the Republican takeover of the White House, had no more illusions about what would follow. "It is now certain that we are about to be engaged in a general civil war between the Northern & Southern states," Stanton wrote to Hutchison on April 15, 1861. "Every one will regret this as a great calamity to the human race." With Virginia and "probably" Maryland likely to join the Confederate states, Washington, sharing borders with both, was vulnerable to Southern occupation, he wrote. "The government will of course strive to protect it but whether successfully or not is perhaps doubtful," he admitted.

"Many persons are preparing to remove from here," he told Hutchison. "I shall remain, and take the chances, feeling a firm faith in the final result…and willing to encounter its risks."

A practical man, Stanton advised his brother-in-law that war, especially conflict in the Ohio and Mississippi Valleys, was likely to be good for local business. "The manufacturing interests of Pittsburgh will I think receive a strong impulse," he predicted. He was right. During the next four years, Pittsburgh and Allegheny County provided heavy arms and ammunition, as well as thousands of volunteers, for Union forces.

Although a longtime Democrat, Stanton became an adviser to Lincoln and then, in 1862, his secretary of war. He was present when Lincoln died on April 15, 1865, the morning after John Wilkes Booth shot him at Ford's Theater. "Now he belongs to the ages," a tearful Stanton said.

A DEMOCRAT BACKS LINCOLN

A "feverish excitement" raised the political temperature in Pittsburgh as news circulated about the opening shots of what many feared would be civil war. In the early morning of Friday, April 12, 1861, Confederate artillery in South Carolina fired on Fort Sumter and the U.S. flag waving above it.

The shelling of Fort Sumter on April 12, 1861, turned at least one Pittsburgh Democrat into a defender of the Union. Image is from *Harper's Pictorial History of the Civil War Part First*. *Courtesy Senator John Heinz History Center.*

"The news of the attack…was received in the city about ten o'clock last night, and created the most feverish excitement," the *Daily Pittsburgh Gazette* reported on Saturday morning. "[H]undreds were slow to credit the rumors, but on receiving assurances of the truth of the reports, the people upon the streets formed in knots discussing the all-absorbing topic of the hour," the paper said. Messengers were "running hither and thither, keeping up communications with the various printing offices, the telegraph office, and other sources of correct information."

A new play, the *Chimney Corner*, had opened at the city's Pittsburgh Theater on Wood Street. It had drawn a large crowd for the Friday evening performance, the newspaper reported. Between the acts, a dispatch was read, announcing the opening of hostilities, which "elicited the wildest enthusiasm, the reader being interrupted by repeated bursts of applause."

Pittsburgh in 1861 had strong economic links to the Mississippi Valley, and many of its residents had roots below the Mason-Dixon line. A significant minority was Democrat and sympathetic to the Southern cause. The Confederate attack on Fort Sumter, which was commanded by Major Robert Anderson, changed at least one theater-goer's view of the situation, the *Gazette* reported: "At the close, a patriotic individual arose in the audience, exclaiming, 'I'm a Democrat! But three cheers for Major Anderson!'"

"The sentiment sent a thrill through the entire audience," the newspaper said.

While headlines in the Republican-leaning *Gazette* simply said, "War Commenced!" and "Surrender Demanded!" the *Pittsburgh Post* was still looking for a peaceful resolution. The lead headlines on its editorial page admitted, "The War Has Begun," but a second commentary urged readers to "Hope on, Hope Ever."

"There is a feeling for Union, both North and South, which even now is having an immense influence upon all classes," the paper said, continuing that "the masses of the people still hope and believe that we shall escape this dire calamity."

The Confederates began shelling Fort Sumter after President Abraham Lincoln affirmed his intentions to resupply its garrison and sent a relief squadron south.

The *Post,* nevertheless, saw reasons for optimism in reports of negotiations between the secessionist South Carolina government and the fort's Union defenders. Confederate president Jefferson Davis would seek "to repress the fighting propensities of Southern chivalry and wait for the more practical course of compromise," the paper predicted.

"If the [Lincoln] administration supplies Fort Sumter, the President of the seceded states will probably make no opposition," the *Post* concluded.

The newspaper was a poor prognosticator.

Southern gunners already had shelled supply boats from the U.S. Navy's small flotilla when it arrived at Charleston. The Union ships then sat helpless outside the harbor, observing the fall of Fort Sumter.

Speaking on April 13, the day that the Federal garrison surrendered, LeRoy Pope Walker, the Confederate secretary of war, predicted the secessionists' flag soon could wave over Washington, D.C., as well.

Quoted in a story from the Confederacy's first capital in Montgomery, Alabama, Walker warned that occupation of Washington would follow if the Lincoln administration didn't recognize Southern independence. His remarks were published in the April 15, 1861 edition of the *Gazette.*

The story that the fort had surrendered was not confirmed in Pittsburgh until the afternoon of April 14. News that the Federal fort had been given up "produced a painfully depressing effect upon all classes," the *Gazette* reported the next morning. "Here and there were to be found a few madcaps (to use no harsher term)—men who sympathize with the Rebels and traitors of the South and quietly cackle over the disgrace which robbery and treason have brought upon the flag of our glorious country!" the newspaper said. "Such men, thank heaven, are very few in this community."

Bulletin boards erected outside newspaper and telegraph offices provided people with the most up-to-date news on the start of the Civil War. Image from *Harper's Pictorial History of the Civil War Part First. Courtesy Senator John Heinz History Center.*

The *Gazette* urged Pittsburgh residents to attend a city hall meeting that night "to confer together upon the state of the country." All the chairs were removed from the assembly room to allow as many as five thousand people to crowd into the building, the newspaper reported the next day. "The venerable Judge WILKINS—a gentleman perhaps as old as the

Constitution itself—was called from his retirement to preside over the meeting," the story said. "The appearance of this venerable citizen and ardent patriot elicited the loudest applause, and he advanced to respond amid the wildest enthusiasm."

Blaming crowded conditions, the *Gazette*'s reporter apologized for not being able to provide a transcript of Wilkins's remarks: "Having no facilities for reporting, we could not take notes and must content ourselves with presenting one or two thoughts from memory."

Regarding the age of Judge William Wilkins, the writer did not exaggerate. Born in December 1779, Wilkins turned eight in 1787, the year the U.S. Constitution was written. A former federal judge, congressman, senator and U.S. secretary of war, he was eighty-one when he addressed the city hall crowd.

While Wilkins and other speakers emphasized defense of the Union, former Allegheny County judge Peter Shannon raised the issue of slavery as a cause of the war. Referring to "the miserable attempt of the Southern traitors to build up a republic on the basis of slavery," he said that "they might as well attempt to build a fire upon the snow-capped summit of the Alps."

The *Gazette* that day also sought to reassure readers about the loyalty of a local militia unit called the Duquesne Greys. Some of its members had fallen under suspicion, in part because one of their officers, Captain David Campbell, was "a consistent Democrat," the newspaper said. It reported, however, that Campbell had proved himself "an ardent patriot" and that the evidence could be found in his having volunteered his military skills to Pennsylvania's Republican governor, Andrew Curtin. "Those who were disposed to cast suspicion upon the Greys as a company will undoubtedly have their minds disabused by this cheering announcement," the paper concluded.

ARTILLERY PIECES FROM FORT PITT FOUNDRY PASS A BIG TEST

Testing, or "proving," Pittsburgh-made artillery was combined with alfresco dining by local businessmen and their wives during the summer of 1861. On June 5, 1861, crews transported ten cannons, called "columbiads," and four mortars by train from the city to a "proving ground" across the Allegheny River from Tarentum. There the guns produced at the Fort Pitt Foundry were subjected to daylong tests.

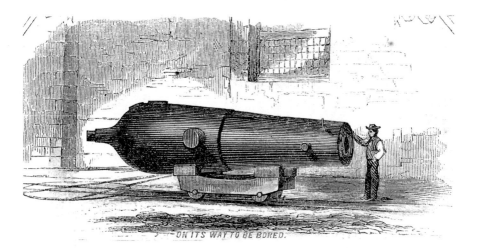

Engraving published in the August 23, 1862 edition of *Harper's Weekly* shows a cannon ready for boring at Pittsburgh's Fort Pitt Foundry. *Courtesy Senator John Heinz History Center.*

"Some experiments were also made to ascertain the effect of projectiles on heavy iron plates," according to a next-day story in the *Pittsburgh Dispatch*. "The experiments on the iron plate, together with the novelty of the Government proof [meaning test], attracted quite a large party, chiefly gentlemen connected with the iron interest," the story said. "A number of ladies also accompanied the party, for whose special delectation the aid of a city confectioner had been called in to prepare a banquet 'al fresco.'

"Several lawyers and 'gentlemen of leisure' were also added to the party, engrafting the lighter amusement of an impromptu picnic on the graver business of Uncle Sam," the report went on.

Such weapons tests were especially important in the opening months of the Civil War as Pittsburgh's workshops, foundries and "manufactories" geared up to supply the Union forces with weapons, ammunition and uniforms. The site of the former proving ground is now private property, according to local historian Arthur B. Fox, who has identified the spot. Although the location was more than twenty miles upriver from Pittsburgh's Golden Triangle, the area was by no means wilderness in the nineteenth century.

The site lacked "a large extent of waste country or a body of water...on which the balls or shells may fall without risking life," the story said. Mortars were usually tested by angling their barrels at forty-five degrees, but the *Dispatch* story said that the weapons for these tests were aimed almost parallel to the ground in an effort to keep spent rounds from landing close to nearby houses.

Fort Pitt Foundry produced mortars like this ten-inch model, now in a Lancaster warehouse. *Courtesy Darrell Sapp of the* Pittsburgh Post-Gazette.

Later tests included mortar firings at near point-blank range—a mere one hundred yards—at iron plates of various thicknesses. "The plates were invariably hit, and generally at approximately the center, which would not have disgraced many riflemen," the reporter wrote.

Gun crews then carried out similar checks on the eight-inch columbiads, smoothbore cannons that fired sixty-four-pound balls. During the proving ground trials, one of the targets for two of the guns was a five-inch-thick iron sheet. When the smoke cleared away after one test firing, observers found that two trees had been toppled and the plate had been hit twice and broken in half. "The result of all the firing proves that at short range no ordinary, or practicable iron sheeting would resist the power of a columbiad shot," the reporter concluded.

That conclusion, however, would be proved at least partially wrong nine months later. In March 1862, the Union's *Monitor* and the Confederate's *Merrimac*, both ironclads, battled each other to a draw at the mouth of the James River in Virginia. The results of that otherwise minor engagement showed that iron plate could be very effective in protecting ships and their crews from cannon fire. In the years that followed, navies around the world rapidly converted their fleets from wood to iron.

PENNSYLVANIANS SHOW MERCY
TO REBEL SUPPORTER

When the Civil War opened, the South began thirty-five miles west of Pittsburgh. In June 1861, what is now the northern panhandle of West Virginia was still part of Virginia, a state that had recently joined the Confederacy. Many residents of the state's northern and western counties, however, were pro-Union.

In Grafton, an important railroad town on the Baltimore & Ohio line, western Virginia men had formed a militia unit, called the Grafton Guards, to protect their town and oppose the Rebels. One of their number, Thornsbury Bailey Brown, died of a gunshot wound on May 22, killed by a Confederate sentry. Brown is often described as the first Union soldier to have died in battle.

Facing a much larger Confederate force commanded by Colonel George Porterfield, the Grafton Guards soon fled by rail to Wheeling, a stronghold of anti-secessionists. Porterfield was able to hold the town for about a week. He withdrew farther south to Philippi as Union forces advanced. Those troops were mostly from Ohio and Indiana, but they also included a regiment of western Virginians. The *Daily Pittsburgh Gazette* reported on June 8 that Pennsylvania cavalry from Fayette and Greene Counties also had helped clear the "ruffians and marauders" out of Grafton.

The source for what the newspaper called a "most interesting narration of the expedition" was Colonel Daniel R. Davidson, a businessman from Connellsville. "Everywhere along the road, from the Pennsylvania line to Grafton, the Pennsylvanians were received with the most cordial and enthusiastic welcome," the *Gazette* said. "[T]hey were met by a band of little girls, dressed in red, white and blue, preceded by a band of music," Davidson told the newspaper. "No secessionists were to be seen."

The militiamen found one exception: an elderly man on horseback whose saddlebags contained eleven clean shirts. A neighbor identified the rider as "an old Secessioner." When the cavalry reached Grafton with its prisoner, "a lot of pretty rough fellows came up and were for pitching in and taking summary measures with the old man," the *Gazette* told readers. Davidson, however, stepped in. "The next thing was to institute a military court, which gave him a regular and fair trial," the paper said. "It was clearly proven that he was a Secessionist; that he had two sons in the Rebel army; and that he was on his way to see them. Of course he was found guilty."

His punishment, however, was mild: "It was proposed to the old gentleman that if he would solemnly swear to support the Constitution of the United States they would set him at liberty." He agreed. "Tears ran down the old man's cheeks while he took the solemn pledge," the *Gazette* reported. "Everybody shook him by the hand, and even the 'roughs,' who a little while before were going to kill him, now clustered around him in boisterous kindness."

Even before Virginia's secession had been ratified, western Virginians had met in Wheeling in May 1861 to debate formation of a new state that would stay in the Union. In June, delegates assembled again in Wheeling and declared themselves to be the real government of Virginia. In October, a West Virginia statehood referendum passed, and a new constitution was drawn up and ratified in 1862. West Virginia was admitted to the Union in 1863.

PITTSBURGH REGIMENTS DEMAND BETTER EQUIPMENT

Harrisburg's Camp Curtin, set up by and named for Pennsylvania governor Andrew Curtin, did not meet the standards of Colonel Samuel Black, commander of the Sixty-second Pennsylvania Volunteers, when the regiment shipped out from Pittsburgh in the summer of 1861.

So Black "scoured the country around" the state capital and found "the most beautiful camp ground in the country" for his men, according to a report in the August 14, 1861 edition of the *Daily Pittsburgh Gazette*. The men set up their tents and dug their latrines on farmland belonging to Simon Cameron just east of Harrisburg. Cameron was a Pennsylvania politician recently named secretary of war by Abraham Lincoln, and the soldiers named the site Camp Cameron in his honor.

As was common during the Civil War, the report to the newspaper on the activities of the Sixty-second was submitted by a soldier in the unit, identified only by his initials: J.T.C. "Our tents are of good material, afford ample protection against rain, and are situated just west of a fine woodland of stately forest trees," he reported. A nearby stream provided water for bathing and washing clothes. The camp was laid out with names familiar to soldiers from Pittsburgh and Allegheny City, now the North Side. They included East and West Commons and Federal and Liberty Streets. Their commander, Pittsburgh-born Samuel Black, had fought in the Mexican-American War and later became territorial governor of Nebraska. He was a no-nonsense officer. "No obscene language or swearing whatever is tolerated," J.T.C. wrote. "Discipline of a very strict character is enforced, and six or seven men are detailed every morning to clear away all rubbish, 'level the ground,' pull up roots &c." Secretary Cameron himself made a brief visit to the camp, "promising to send our uniforms, and equipments, &c, from Washington city directly."

Conditions were much less promising during the early months of the war for another local regiment: the Ninth Pennsylvania Reserve Corps. The unit, primarily Allegheny County volunteers, was assigned to Camp Tennally, northwest of Washington, D.C. The Pennsylvania legislature had promised the men that they "were to be equipped in a superior manner," a soldier correspondent wrote in the August 17 edition of the *Gazette*. He identified himself with the single initial "K." Instead, "they were armed with old Harper's Ferry altered muskets, the general appearance of which would indicate that they were manufactured by some backwoods blacksmith and wagon maker," he wrote. "Not one bayonet out of every dozen can be fixed or unfixed in under fifteen minutes," he claimed. He wrote that the musket barrels were so thin that "after firing three or four rounds they become so hot, it is almost impossible to hold them." In an effort to cover up the defects in the outmoded weapons, the muskets had been given a fresh coat of paint.

The inadequacies of their guns placed the men in danger from nearby Confederate forces, the story said. "I really wished a few days since, when on picket duty, almost in sight of the enemy, that Curtin himself occupied the position of the men in the ranks," K wrote. The Allegheny County men risked being "picked off at the distance of a thousand feet, when our beautiful, well painted muskets would not reach half that distance." K closed with a challenge to Pennsylvania legislators and the governor: "If Gov. Curtin wishes to redeem his character…let him at once procure with the millions at his disposal, ten thousand stands of improved arms."

Chapter 3

Getting to Know the Players

THE *GAZETTE* INTRODUCES MRS. LINCOLN

Curiosity about presidential spouses is not a twenty-first-century phenomenon. The election of 1860, in which Abraham Lincoln became president, placed Mary Todd Lincoln in the national spotlight as well. On March 4, 1861, the day that her husband was inaugurated as the nation's sixteenth president, the *Daily Pittsburgh Gazette* had a story describing the appearance and character of the new first lady. The next morning, March 5, the *Pittsburgh Post* ran a shorter report on Lincoln's vice president, Hannibal Hamlin, and his second, much younger, wife, Ellen.

An anonymous *New York Times* correspondent who had traveled with the president-elect and his family on their trip from Springfield, Illinois, to Washington wrote the lengthy feature on Mary Lincoln. Previous newspaper reports had made Mrs. Lincoln out to be either a Roman goddess or a frontier hick, the story said. Those diverse views of Mrs. Lincoln appeared to depend primarily on whether the writers backed or opposed her husband's election.

The "Portrait" in the *Gazette* first sought to dispel misconceptions about her: "Mrs. Lincoln does not chew snuff, does not dress in outré style, does not walk 'al a Zouave,' does not use profane language, nor does she on any occasion, public or private, kick up shindies." Journalists who had compared Mrs. Lincoln's walk to that of a Zouave had meant to be insulting. Zouaves originally were French North African soldiers who wore baggy, brightly colored, Eastern-influenced uniforms. The style later was adopted by military units from both sides during the Civil War. To "kick up a shindy"

Gazette readers in 1861 were assured that Mary Todd Lincoln did not dress like a Zouave soldier. *Courtesy the* Pittsburgh Post-Gazette.

was no compliment either. It was a nineteenth-century term for starting quarrels or causing commotion.

"Her form inclines to stoutness, but is well fashioned and comely, while her hands and feet are really beautiful," the reporter wrote of Mrs. Lincoln. Her lovely extremities and her "well-shaped ear" indicated that "she has come from a race of people who were well born," he concluded. Her blue eyes, non-Grecian nose, expressive mouth and rounded chin supported his conclusion that "she is a decided—not obstinate—woman."

Lincoln's vice president, a former senator from Maine, was described in the *Post*, despite the newspaper's usual hostility to Republican politicians, as "one of nature's noblemen." It compared Hamlin favorably with longtime Massachusetts senator Daniel Webster. The story's unnamed writer was unusual in that she was described as a "lady correspondent."

"I must not forget to say of Mrs. Hamlin what one lady is loath to allow of another, that she is right pretty," the reporter wrote. "From Mrs.

Hamlin's youthful demeanor and her husband's devotion she is evidently a second spouse…she is petite with auburn hair and hazel eyes." According to the correspondent, Mrs. Hamlin also had "a sunshiny smile and unpretending manners."

At twenty-five, Ellen Hamlin was half the age of her fifty-one-year-old husband when he became vice president. Replaced by Democrat Andrew Johnson on a unity ticket in 1864, Hamlin returned to the U.S. Senate, representing Maine for another twelve years. He died in 1891. Ellen Hamlin lived until 1925.

Tragedy dogged Mrs. Lincoln, on the other hand, who saw her husband mortally wounded and buried three of her four children. Concerned that she might kill herself, her surviving son, Robert, had his mother briefly committed to an insane asylum. After being released into the care of her sister, Mary Todd Lincoln died in Springfield, Illinois, in 1882.

YOUNG ABE'S UNLIKELY DUEL

Abraham Lincoln once said a single line of verse from English poet Thomas Gray could sum up his early years: "The short and simple annals of the Poor." That wasn't near enough information for curious Americans who, in 1861, wanted to know much more about their new president. Apocryphal stories about "Honest Abe" began to pile up like autumn leaves outside the door of a prairie cabin.

The *Daily Pittsburgh Gazette* on November 14, 1861, offered its readers an improbable, but partially accurate, tale of Lincoln's near-comic participation in a duel in 1842. Lincoln, a Whig, had been feuding with the Illinois state auditor, James Shields, and he had written a satirical letter, under the pseudonym Aunt Becca, for a local newspaper. In it, he joked about both his Democratic opponent's policies and his vanity. In his 1995 biography of Lincoln, historian David Herbert Donald writes that Mary Todd, whom Lincoln later would marry, angered Shields even more when she co-authored a second "Aunt Becca" letter to the editor, making fun of the politician's recent romantic misadventures. When Lincoln took responsibility for both letters, Shields challenged him to a fight.

The story about the duel that appeared in the *Gazette* appears to be wrong in claiming that Lincoln had insulted Shields in verse, not prose. But the story was accurate in noting that "there were those who believed that the

Abraham Lincoln, as a young man, was one of the principals in an embarrassing duel. *Courtesy Senator John Heinz History Center.*

verses had been indited by fairer hands than Lincoln's…and it was impossible for him to back out by throwing the responsibility on another, and that other a lady." (Indite is an archaic term meaning to write.)

Dueling was illegal in Illinois, so the two men and their seconds agreed to meet at a spot known as Bloody Island in the middle of the Mississippi River in neighboring Missouri. As the party challenged to the duel, Lincoln had his choice of weapons. He selected broadswords. At six feet four inches tall, and with long, strong arms, Lincoln had a much longer reach than Shields, who was five foot nine. According to the *Gazette*, Lincoln imposed other conditions as well, such as between the combatants "there should be erected a rail barrier four and a half feet high, and all blows to be exchanged over this barrier." Each combatant was "to be at liberty to approach as near the barrier or keep as distant from it as he might choose but not to jump over or go around it."

"These extraordinary terms were at first indignantly rejected, but Mr. Lincoln would offer no others, and Mr. Shields was forced either to accept them or go without a fight," the *Gazette* reported.

Both sides arrived on Bloody Island, but ultimately, there was no face-off. The *Gazette* story said that "just as they were about to engage in the duel, and after the fence had been erected, friends interfered, and the actual fight was prevented."

While the tale adds a great detail to a story about a man well known as a "rail splitter," the rail barrier appears to have no basis in fact. Neither Donald nor historian Daniel Mark Epstein, who wrote a joint biography of Abraham and Mary Todd Lincoln in 2008, mentions any fence in his description of the incident.

An officer of the court, Lincoln remained embarrassed for the rest of his life that he had come close to violating the law by agreeing to a duel. Donald writes that Lincoln was asked about the incident during the Civil War. The president admitted the truth, but he warned his questioner, "If you desire my friendship, you will never mention it again."

GRANT PICKS UP A NICKNAME

General Ulysses S. Grant picked up his nickname—Unconditional Surrender Grant—after Union soldiers under his command captured Fort Donelson, Tennessee, on February 16, 1862. The fort's Confederate commander, General Simon Bolivar Buckner, had asked Grant for "the appointment of Commissioners to agree upon the terms of capitulation," according to a story in the February 19 edition of the *Pittsburgh Post*. Grant and his reply became famous: "No terms except an unconditional and immediate surrender can be accepted," Grant wrote back. "I propose to move immediately upon your works."

Grant's forces captured about twelve thousand Confederates, including Buckner. One larger fish, however, escaped. Fort Donelson's previous commander, former U.S. secretary of war John B. Floyd, had fled, leaving most of his troops behind. Floyd was still notorious in Pittsburgh for his

The *Daily Pittsburgh Gazette* informed readers in February 1862 how U.S. Grant got his nickname. Image from *Harper's Pictorial History of the Civil War Part First. Courtesy Senator John Heinz History Center.*

attempt to ship artillery to the South in 1860. Many Northerners believed that he had planned treason and that the weapons soon would have fallen into the hands of secessionists.

The fort's surrender and Floyd's flight hurt Southern morale. "At first the prisoners were loud in their denunciations of the runaways," according to the *Post*. Some were ready to give up the fight: "Many of them acknowledged the hopelessness of their cause, and intimated their willingness to take the oath of allegiance, and return to their homes."

In a story that appeared a few weeks later, the *Daily Pittsburgh Gazette* printed a report on "trophies" and letters found on the battlefield. The items were picked up by a steamship clerk named Stanton Batchelor, who sent them north to his brother, Captain C.W. Batchelor, Pittsburgh's customs collector. "The most conspicuous of the trophies was a huge knife, called a 'tooth pick,' and forming part of the equipment of the Texas Rangers," according to a March 7 story in the *Gazette*. "The belt is much stained with blood, but the knife does not appear to have been used. The weapon is formidable—nay, frightful looking—but of very rude workmanship.

"Mr. Batchelor also sent a coat from the body of a Rebel found dead on the battlefield…Nothing is known of the unfortunate man who wore it."

The clerk also sent along letters he had scavenged. One, from an "affectionate sister" to her brother, Joe, shows how strong anti-Union feeling was that winter. The woman described her daughter as "the sweetest child in the Confederacy…I'll not [compare] her with any of the little Northern toads." When two other children, Emma and Charlie, got into an argument at supper, the little girl called "Charlie a Yankee, which seemed to insult him grossly…and he told her that she should not call him a plagued Yankee, or…he would throw a fork at her."

Another of the letters, from a Mary O. Todd to her husband W.M. Todd, described economic problems at home and, inadvertently, focused on one of the main causes of the war: slavery. "I have hired Ellen out to John Steel for forty-five dollars and her clothes and doctor bill and taxes," she wrote from Fayetteville, Tennessee. "That is better than keeping her at home."

PITTSBURGH MEETS A FUTURE PRESIDENT

As the country split in two, President Abraham Lincoln was determined to hold onto the border areas, including his native state of Kentucky. "I hope to have God on my side, but I must have Kentucky," he is reported to have said during the early days of the conflict.

James A. Garfield, an Ohio schoolteacher turned lawyer turned soldier, helped him keep it. "When so many incapables…have succeeded in getting themselves pitchforked into Brigadier Generalships, it is an occasional luxury we enjoy to record that a Brigadier General can be made out of different material—of better and sterner stuff," the *Daily Pittsburgh Gazette* reported on February 21, 1862.

Garfield was a colonel when he led a successful campaign in December 1861 and January 1862 to force Confederate general Humphrey Marshall "and his rebel hordes" out of eastern Kentucky. President Lincoln, backed by his new secretary of war Edwin Stanton, nominated Garfield for a general's star on February 19, and the Senate confirmed him the same day.

Garfield, commander of the Forty-second Ohio Regiment, had served as de facto field chief of the Army of the Ohio's Eighteenth Brigade,

War hero James Garfield served both as a general and a member of Congress during the Civil War. Image from *Harper's Pictorial History of the Civil War Part First. Courtesy Senator John Heinz History Center.*

the newspaper said. His superior, Brigadier General Don Carlos Buell, had assigned him the task of securing a critical portion of Kentucky, and troops under Garfield's command threw back Confederate forces from the towns of Paintsville and Prestonburg. While they were not major victories, they came at a time when the North needed heroes. "General Garfield is an earnest man," an anonymous "respected contemporary" wrote in the *Gazette*. "His heart is in the work which he has undertaken, and in no way will he be retarded by a tenderness for the rebels. He is a man of brains, too.

"As for military talent, he has given evidence of that by freeing Eastern Kentucky from the bondage to which the people had been subjected by the secessionists…we have faith in a man like Gen. Garfield, who, if need be, will take off his coat to fight the rebels," the newspaper concluded.

In April 1862, General Garfield led troops reinforcing General Ulysses S. Grant at the Battle of Shiloh in Tennessee. While serving as chief of staff for General William Rosecrans later that same year, he won an Ohio congressional election.

Garfield, a Republican, served nine terms in Congress. He became the GOP's dark-horse candidate for president in 1880, defeating another Civil War general, Democrat Winfield Scott Hancock.

Garfield's time as president was short and sad. After taking office in March 1881, he was wounded by a deranged assassin, Charles Guiteau, on July 2. Guiteau's announced goal was to kill Garfield and make Vice

President Chester Arthur president. Modern authors, including Candice Millard, have argued that Garfield was as much a victim of poor medical care as of Guiteau. In her 2011 book, *Destiny of the Republic*, she describes how Garfield's doctors, rejecting germ theory and the need for sterilization, probed his wounds with unwashed fingers and dirty instruments. Not surprisingly, Garfield's condition worsened, and he died on September 19.

His body rests in a mausoleum in Lake View Cemetery in Cleveland. His home, Lawnfield, in Mentor, Ohio, east of Cleveland, is a National Historic Site. The building was expanded after his death to house the first presidential library. The murdered president has a geographic connection to Pittsburgh. The city's Garfield neighborhood is named for him.

LIFE ECHOES FICTION IN SINGLE CIVIL WAR DEATH

Casualty lists printed in Pittsburgh's newspapers grew longer and longer as the Civil War entered its second year. One of the early victims was Captain Leopold Sahl Jr. The son of a Pittsburgh hotelkeeper, Sahl had volunteered for service with the independent Morehead Cavalry. His unit was organized in Allegheny City in August 1861.

Captain Sahl was on a scouting mission in Virginia's Shenandoah Valley when he was shot, according to the *History of the 18th Regiment Infantry*, published in 1901. He died of his wounds on January 17, 1862. His death and the events that followed echoed to some degree an anonymous "Select Tale" that appeared in the *Pittsburgh Post* on July 3, 1862. "Only One Killed" is a fictional story describing the aftermath of "a reconnaissance, a surprise of the enemy's scouts, a brief sharp engagement, ending successfully" with one killed and three wounded. Reading a newspaper account of the skirmish, the narrator remarks that the trifling casualties make reporting on the incident "hardly worth the cost of a telegram."

The narrator is checked for his words, however: "A pair of sober grey eyes were turned upon my face, and I read in them a silent rebuke for this lightness of speech." When the gray-eyed man asks to take a look at the newspaper, the narrator "saw that his hand trembled a little and that his eyes searched through the sentences…in an eager way," but the newspaper account included no names for the victims.

"I have a son in that company," the gray-eyed man explains as he returns the paper.

The two were riding in a horse-drawn streetcar, and "soon after, the man nodded to the conductor on the car; the check string was pulled, the car stopped and he got out." When the narrator passes that same spot five days later, he sees a funeral wreath on one door. Mr. B——, the gray-eyed man, has lost his only son, Edward.

"Mr. B—— is one of those men who bear things patiently; but he has deep feelings nevertheless," a neighborhood storekeeper says. "That boy was his idol."

"Only one killed," the narrator muses. "How insignificant the fact seemed when the telegraph made this announcement, but what bitterness had followed."

The next day he watches Edward's funeral procession:

> *Of the tens of thousands who had lingered scarcely a moment over the brief telegram…had the imagination of one individual pictured distinctly the solemn scene like this…or given the faintest realization of the sorrow and suffering that lay veiled behind.*
>
> *One, two or three hundred killed or mangled. It is awful to contemplate…Away from every battle-field, from every skirmishing ground, heart chords stretch, in single lines, to as many hearts and homes as there are individuals…each with his own wild fear and anguish.*

Edward's mother had shut herself up in her room since her son's death, and the narrator of "Only One Killed" hints that further sadness likely lay ahead for his survivors. A similar result certainly followed for Pittsburgh's Sahl family.

Six months to the day after Captain Sahl's death, the *Post* reported on the passing of his father: "Col. Leopold Sahl, one of our oldest and most respected German citizens…died yesterday after an illness of some two weeks."

"Col. Sahl leaves a wife but no children, his only son, Capt. Leopold Sahl Jr., having been killed in an engagement with the Rebels in Virginia," the July 17 story said.

Father and son are buried in St. Mary's Cemetery in Pittsburgh's Lawrenceville neighborhood.

Chapter 4

On the Homefront

BOTH SIDES CALL ON GOD'S AID AT THANKSGIVING

As it became clearer that the Civil War would not end quickly, both U.S. president Abraham Lincoln and Confederate president Jefferson Davis issued fall proclamations linked to the deadly conflict.

Davis selected November 15, 1861, as "a day of national humiliation and prayer." He called on residents across the South "to repair on that day to their homes and usual places of public worship, and to implore the blessings of almighty God upon our people, that he may give us victories over our enemies." Those enemies in the North should be humbled, Davis wrote, with their efforts ending in "confusion and shame."

Pennsylvania governor Andrew Curtin joined seventeen of his gubernatorial colleagues in selecting November 28 as Thanksgiving. His proclamation set aside the day "for solemn thanksgiving to God for having prepared our corn and watered our furrows." Curtin also asked "that our beloved country may have deliverance from these great and apparent dangers…and that He will mercifully still the outrage of perverse, violent, unruly and rebellious people…and give them grace that they may see the error of their ways."

President Lincoln joined state officials and ordered municipal and federal employees in Washington to halt operations on that same day, "in order that the officers of the government may partake in the ceremonies." Russell Errett, editor of the *Daily Pittsburgh Gazette*, wrote on Thursday, November

Confederate president Jefferson Davis called for "a day of national humiliation and prayer." *Courtesy U.S. National Archives.*

28, that there were many things Pennsylvanians should be thankful for even as "a war of frightful character" continued. The state had not been invaded, business was prospering and, not surprisingly, demand for labor was rising, he said. "A bountiful harvest had crowned the labors of the husbandman, and food is plenty and cheap…and we can look forward to the coming winter without apprehension of any unwonted suffering among the poor." Like most Pittsburgh residents, the newspaper's reporters and printers had that day off, and no paper was published the next day.

Allegheny's First Presbyterian Church was the scene of a holiday concert that drew praise afterward from an anonymous newspaper reviewer. "The music was all sacred and consisted principally of anthems taken from joyous and thanksgiving psalms, and other selections from the unmatched poetry of the Bible," the *Gazette*'s story said. "Before the singing of each piece a brief, comprehensive and fervidly eloquent exposition…of the piece immediately to follow was given by the Rev. Elliott Swift.

"The effect of the frequent and rapid alteration between excellent music and genuine eloquence from a man whose voice is music, was singularly impressive," according to the November 30 story. "The church was very full, and although no audible applause was given—for it would have been out of place—yet the countenances of all testified how well they were pleased."

While previous presidents had declared days of thanksgiving, it was not until 1863 that Lincoln proclaimed an annual holiday to be celebrated on the last Thursday of November. At the urging of retailers during the Great Depression, Franklin Roosevelt switched the date to the fourth Thursday, a move that extended the holiday shopping season.

CONFEDERATE SYMPATHIZER FORCED TO LEAVE

Though Abraham Lincoln had called Allegheny County a "banner county of the state," the region still had a number of Southern sympathizers. A letter published in the *Gazette* on March 17, 1862, however, showed that life in wartime Allegheny County had become more perilous for them.

Lee A. Beckham was a Virginia native who grew up in Allegheny City and had been in business there since the late 1840s. He had also been an unsuccessful Democratic candidate in 1860 for the state legislature. "After the election of Mr. Lincoln, my sympathies being with my native region, I did not hesitate to advocate the Southern cause on all proper occasions," Beckham wrote in a letter to Virginia governor John Letcher.

Bayard Taylor, a war correspondent for the *New York Tribune*, found Beckham's letter "among the rubbish at Manassas," according to the *Gazette* report. Taylor had been imbedded with General George McClellan's Union army when Federal forces advanced into Virginia in March 1862.

Beckham, the Pittsburgh newspaper said, was "well known to our citizens" when he "left the city very mysteriously last spring."

In his letter, Beckham wrote that he had spent about three weeks in Venango County, where he "had some oil interests," and returned to his Allegheny City home a few days after the fall of Fort Sumter. He then found suspicions about his loyalties so strong that one of his friends had fallen under a cloud after "he was seen in conversation with me."

"The [Allegheny] lampposts were provided with ropes to hang what they called traitors," Beckham wrote, adding that he had been coerced into proving his Union loyalty by raising funds for the war effort. "They finally served a final notice on me to raise the Federal flag and gave me 48 hours to do so or abide the consequences," his letter said. "At the earnest entreaty of my friends, I at last consented to leave the city rather than meet what would have been my fate at the expiration of the time allowed me."

He, his wife and their child decamped to the home of a brother-in-law in Maryland, a border state that remained neutral during the war. "I had to abandon my property and my business," he stated. "From a condition of comparative ease and affluence, my family are now dependent for support upon what I can earn."

He told Governor Letcher that he was willing to do any work "that may be required of an honest and energetic man." He asked the governor to "aid me to some position where I can do something to support my family, and at the same time, to the extent of my ability, serve my native State."

Beckham had some powerful friends, including a former U.S. congressman named James Barbour. Attached to Beckham's letter was a recommendation from Barbour, by that time a major in the Confederate army. Beckham and his family deserved consideration, Barbour wrote, because of the "heavy misfortunes which his loyalty to his native State has brought on him and them."

WHAT WAR BETWEEN BROTHERS REALLY MEANS

A correspondent for the *Daily Pittsburgh Gazette* offered firsthand evidence that the Civil War was literally a fight between brothers.

The anonymous reporter was interviewing Colonel Edward P. Fyffe, commander of the Twenty-sixth Ohio Infantry, just after the Battle of Shiloh. The two-day fight in southwestern Tennessee on April 7–8, 1862, was the bloodiest clash thus far in the year-old war. Casualties on both sides during the engagement, also known as the Battle of Pittsburg Landing, totaled more than twenty-four thousand.

Colonel Fyffe "directed my attention to his adjutant, a remarkable prepossessing officer and as fine a specimen of a man as one would meet in a brigade," the Pittsburgh journalist wrote in a story that appeared on

April 22. As Union troops set up their camps, they were ordered to bury any enemy bodies found on the site. "Passing the regiment a few minutes before, I observed the 26th at this business, and also noticed a man half covered, with his name in Indian [*sic*] ink upon his arm," the story said. Soldiers wore no dog tags to identify them if they were killed or wounded, so some pinned paper notes with their names to their coats or used water-resistant India ink to mark their skin.

The dead Confederate was among seven corpses awaiting burial. "The men were tiring of shoveling, when one of them observing the name on the arm, called to the Adjutant to 'come and see some of his relatives.'"

"He had passed that particular corpse perhaps 50 times on that day," the reporter wrote. "Now he appeared disturbed.

"He look at the bared arm, saw the old scars, and turning to the men around said, 'Yes, he is my brother.'"

The *Gazette* correspondent stayed to watch the burial.

"The Adjutant exhibited no softness, but his manner betrayed his mental suffering," the story said. "The men lifted the dead rebel very respectfully indeed. They dug a grave, a deep one, and after laying the corpse out regularly on a tent on the ground, they buried it alone." The Northern soldiers used a tree at the head of the grave as a living marker, carving the words "To the memory of" and the Confederate's name into it. The adjutant, who served as an administrative assistant to the colonel, told the reporter his brother had headed to California two years earlier. The family later learned that he had stopped in Missouri, a border state with a population divided between Union supporters and secessionists. Finding his sibling's body on the battlefield was "the first news the living brother has heard of him since."

The same *Gazette* report also described a sharpshooter from Company B of the Seventy-seventh Pennsylvania Volunteer Infantry, who took a more cold-blooded approach to his battlefield duties.

After a Confederate rifleman had fired three times at the company captain, the officer "had ventured to try his hand on the man," but his pistol misfired. The captain, "who had too many things to attend to at that particular juncture," then ordered the sharpshooter, referred to by the initial "D," to "take him down." Biding his time, the soldier fired at the Southerner. "Suddenly, the secesh [fell] heavily after throwing up his hands."

Later that day, Union forces drove the Confederates to retreat, and the sharpshooter walked over to his slain enemy. "Private D picked the man up, enquired how he felt, propped him against a tree, and taking a button off his jacket as a souvenir, proceeded in search of other game."

"The whole line saw private D do this and another thing similar to it in a very few minutes afterwards," the correspondent wrote. "Sharp shooting is nothing but a sort of a game after all."

COOKED CAT COMPETES FOR READERS' ATTENTION

Not all newspaper stories centered on the progress of the Civil War. According to a story that appeared on March 5, 1862, in the *Daily Pittsburgh Gazette* and stirred up much attention, an angry Allegheny City brewer sought culinary revenge on one of his former customers.

J.E. Heinrichs claimed that he and a half dozen other men had been invited to Sunday dinner at the home of Conrad Eberhart. Meats for the meal included goose and rabbit. According to the newspaper report, Eberhart had urged all his guests to be sure to try the roast rabbit. The host later told some of the diners that what they had consumed had been roast cat. Eberhart was charged under an 1834 state statute that forbid "serving unwholesome food in any inn, tavern or place for the public accommodation of man and beast," according to the story.

Heinrichs, his alleged victim, owned a beer hall and restaurant on Federal Street in what was then Allegheny City. Heinrichs told the court that his dinner host held a grudge against him after Heinrichs stopped buying products from Eberhart's brewery. Testimony was heard by an Allegheny alderman—the nineteenth-century equivalent of a magisterial district judge—named Scott, and the *Gazette* reported that the unusual charges in the case attracted a large, irreverent crowd.

"A good deal of merriment was elicited during the trial, which was heightened by one of the spectators with a cat under his arm," the newspaper said. The trapped feline "kept up a constant caterwauling" each time its owner pinched its tail.

One of the guests, Henry Sieger, said his "supper tasted very good...I got plenty of the rabbit." Diner Louis Kaufmann was more suspicious. "I knew the meat on the table was not a rabbit," he said, but he "could not swear that it was a cat." Eberhart's sister, Laura, told the alderman the animal her brother brought her to prepare "had every appearance of a rabbit." She said she had followed a traditional recipe, soaking the meat "in vinegar, salt and onions for two or three days previous to the supper."

Her testimony also hit at the applicability of the law under which her brother was charged: "My brother does not keep an eating house" and "sells nothing but lager beer."

The most damaging testimony came from dinner guest Amanio Meyer, who said Eberhart had beckoned him over after the meal and told him, "Do you know what you ate? You have eaten a cat!"

"He said he was 'glad that he came it over Heinrichs,'" Meyer told the court. He said that he hadn't paid anything for his supper, which "tasted middling good."

Alderman Scott found Eberhart guilty of the charge and fined him $6—the equivalent of about $134 in modern currency. But the brewer's legal woes were not at an end, according to a March 8 story in the *Pittsburgh Post*. Heinrichs's lawyer, J.H. Whitesell, announced that his client was suing his supper host for civil damages of $10,000. That amount is equal to about $224,000 today, based on changes to the consumer price index.

Newspapers over the next few days carried nothing more about the civil lawsuit, but stories about the original trial attracted the eye of at least one out-of-town editor looking for lighter fare during the dark days of the Civil War. The *Brooklyn Daily Eagle* published its version of "a novel case [that] is exciting attention in Pittsburgh" on March 14, 1862.

ALLEGHENY ARSENAL EXPLODES

Negligence was behind the deadly explosion at the Allegheny Arsenal—at least, that was the conclusion of a cold case coroner's jury that met 150 years after the event.

The multiple blasts and fire on September 17, 1862, killed seventy-eight people, mostly young women and girls. They had been assembling ammunition cartridges at the arsenal, located in what was then the Pittsburgh suburb of Lawrenceville.

It was the worst civilian disaster of the Civil War, but the story was overshadowed outside Pittsburgh by news of a great battle at Antietam Creek, Maryland. Almost twenty-three thousand Union and Confederate soldiers were killed, wounded or missing in that one-day fight.

What were believed initially to be "exaggerated reports" of deaths and injuries at the United States arsenal in Lawrenceville turned out to be even worse than imagined. "So great was the force of the explosion that fragments

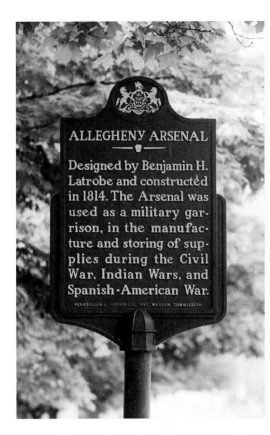

ALLEGHENY ARSENAL

Designed by Benjamin H. Latrobe and constructéd in 1814. The Arsenal was used as a military garrison, in the manufacture and storing of supplies during the Civil War, Indian Wars, and Spanish-American War.

PENNSYLVANIA HISTORICAL AND MUSEUM COMMISSION

Seventy-eight people, mostly young women and girls, died when the Allegheny Arsenal exploded in September 1862. A leafy Pittsburgh park now occupies the site. *Courtesy Bill Wade of the* Pittsburgh Post-Gazette.

from the laboratory were thrown hundreds of feet," the *Pittsburgh Post* reported on September 18, the morning after the disaster. "Shreds of clothing were found in the treetops."

Reporters from both the *Post* and the rival *Daily Pittsburgh Gazette* provided on-the-scene descriptions that call to mind some of the destruction that followed the September 11, 2001 terrorist attacks. "Of the main building nothing remained but a heap of smoking debris," the *Post* reporter wrote. "The ground about was strewn with fragments of charred wood, torn clothing, bails, caps, grape shot, exploded shells, shoes, fragments of dinner baskets belonging to the inmates, steel springs from the girls' hoop skirts, cartridge paper, sheet iron, melted lead."

The arsenal had been founded in 1814, and munitions were made and stored there by government workers for the next one hundred years. During the Civil War, its mostly young, female workforce produced many kinds of artillery shells and cartridges for the Union army. Most workers were girls because they were believed to be more dexterous and diligent. The *Gazette* said boys had "been discharged some time since, they being deemed more careless than the girls."

Both papers included graphic details.

"In some parts, where the heat was intense, nothing but whitened bones could be seen," the *Gazette* said. "The steel bands remaining from the hoop skirts of the unfortunate girls marked the place where many of them perished."

The crowd of spectators drawn by the noise and fire was "immense and constantly increased," the *Post* reported. "Some were satisfied with a brief stay in that sickening atmosphere…but others [were] lingering about, giving assistance where they could and talking over the horrible details."

Not everyone was there to help. Exploding munitions had left many victims with shrapnel and gunshot wounds. "In the side of another girl, seven Minié balls were discovered," the *Gazette* reported. "These balls…were all picked out and carried off by curiosity seekers."

By the next day, the newspapers had begun speculating on possible causes. "One account says it was occasioned by the explosion of a shell, a number of which, being sent off for shipment, fell and caused a concussion," the *Post* reported. "Others allege that it was occasioned by friction of some powder from one of three barrels unloaded upon the porch of the laboratory."

"A young lady, with whom we conversed, and who was employed in the building, states that the explosion was caused by a boy, who let fall a shell which he was carrying," the *Gazette* said.

An Allegheny County coroner's jury was convened two days after the explosion to look into what happened.

Witness J.R. Frick had been delivering different types of powder to the various workrooms in the laboratory where armaments were assembled that afternoon. "I saw a fire [in the] powder on the ground between the wheels of the wagon and the [laboratory] porch," he said, according to the September 20 edition of the *Gazette*. "The powder in the roadway…evidently ignited from the fore wheel of my wagon." He also said he recalled seeing several barrels of powder that had been left uncovered.

Both the 1862 original coroner's jury and the cold case jury, which met September 15, 2012, at Pittsburgh's Senator John Heinz History Center, reached similar conclusions. The physical cause was loose gunpowder, most likely ignited by a spark from an iron wagon wheel or a horseshoe. Both juries found that responsibility for that unsafe condition rested with the army officers in charge of the facility, but a follow-up military investigation in 1862 declined to assign guilt.

Most of the dead were buried a few blocks away in Allegheny Cemetery. Catholic victims were interred in nearby St. Mary's Cemetery.

Located between Thirty-ninth and Fortieth Streets, the site of the explosion has been converted into Arsenal Park. A commemorative plaque installed in 1965 by the Historical Society of Western Pennsylvania recalls the tragedy.

The 150th anniversary of the disaster was marked in September 2012 with a public reading of the names of all seventy-eight victims at the Heinz

Lawrenceville historian Tom Powers and former Allegheny County coroner Cyril Wecht hold up a drawing that shows the layout of Allegheny Arsenal buildings during the Civil War. The pair took part in a 2012 cold case inquest into the causes of the 1862 disaster. *Courtesy Tony Tye of the* Pittsburgh Post-Gazette.

History Center. At least one person at the event had a personal interest in the commemoration. Marie Gray of Pittsburgh's Shadyside neighborhood was the great-great-granddaughter of Mary "May" Collins, who was twenty-seven when she was killed in the disaster.

Mrs. Gray's father, the late Robert J. Scheib Sr., had kept the memory of May Collins alive within their family. The victims did not receive a hero's acknowledgement at the time of their deaths, Mrs. Gray said, so it was appropriate to honor them at an anniversary tribute.

NEWSPAPERS BATTLE OVER EMANCIPATION'S MEANING

A Union victory at Antietam gave President Abraham Lincoln the opening he had been looking for.

On September 22, 1862, five days after the battle in Maryland, he issued the Emancipation Proclamation. He had been urged by his cabinet to wait for a battlefield victory before announcing the major shift in administration policy. Acting on his own authority as president of a country at war, he

Lincoln, discussing emancipation with his cabinet, was the subject of a Civil War–era drawing. *Courtesy Senator John Heinz History Center.*

decreed that on January 1, 1863, "all persons held as slaves within any State [where] the people…shall then be in rebellion against the United States, shall be then, thenceforward and forever free."

While Lincoln's legal reasoning cited military necessity—he sought to deprive the Southern states of a critical source of labor—the president's political friends and foes grasped that bigger issues were at stake.

"Thank God!" Russell Errett, the editor of the *Daily Pittsburgh Gazette*, wrote the next day. "That one brave, needed, emphatic word has been spoken at last! Long expected and long coming, it is all the more welcome, now that it has come."

That word was "free."

The *Gazette*, a supporter of Lincoln and the Republican Party, had been brawling in print with the *Pittsburgh Post* since the war began a year and a half earlier. The *Post* had been the longtime local voice of the Democracy, as the Democratic Party referred to itself.

While the *Gazette* compared Lincoln's action to the Magna Carta, the *Post* was scornful. "Taking experience as our guide, we can see nothing resulting from this proclamation but evil to our cause," *Post* editor James P. Barr wrote on September 25. Lincoln was under the control of Northern radicals, and the president's proclamation was likely to "produce greater unanimity and spirit among the rebels." The *Post* warned that his proclamation also could bring about the Southerners' nightmare scenario: slave uprisings. Unless the war came to a speedy conclusion, the Confederacy would face "the brutality and savage ferocity of infuriated thousands [of slaves], following the bloody instructions of Northern fanaticism."

A few days earlier, on September 23, the *Post* had quoted from the last letter sent home by U.S. Army captain E.R. Brady, a Jefferson County soldier recently killed in action. Government policy "in agitating acts of confiscation and emancipation only gives something to nerve the enemy to fight against us," he wrote to his mother at home in Brookville. He and many of his comrades enlisted to put down a rebellion, and they were disheartened that the new goal was "to free the negro."

"The army is opposed to this and would like to see the negro question stopped," he wrote. "And unless it is speedily done, we must console ourselves with the thought that the country has been ruined and made bankrupt through the imbecility of our people."

About 180,000 black men, including many former slaves, enlisted in Union forces during the Civil War. Engraving from *Harper's Pictorial History of the Civil War Part Second* shows quarters for what were called U.S. Colored Troops. *Courtesy Senator John Heinz History Center.*

The *Gazette*, on the other hand, predicted quick benefits from Lincoln's action:

> *The result of this order is to give immediate freedom to all slaves who have come, or who may hereafter come, into the lines of our army, or who may, now or hereafter, come under the control of the government of the United States. This is virtually an invitation to all slaves in the Rebel States to come within our lines and be immediately free. That thousands and tens of thousands will avail themselves of this grand invitation there can be no doubt. Heaven be praised! There is to be no more man hunting—and no returning of men to bondage!*

Thousands of black men, including many former slaves who had fled Confederate-controlled areas, joined the United States Colored Troops. By the war's end, black units totaling almost 180,000 soldiers made up about 10 percent of the Union army.

FRIENDLY GUNFIRE GREETS LINCOLN'S PROCLAMATION

Pittsburgh greeted with gunshots the announcement that President Abraham Lincoln had signed the Emancipation Proclamation on January 1, 1863.

The volleys were not fired in anger but in celebration, according to the *Daily Pittsburgh Gazette*. "The numerous friends of the Emancipation message in this city, expressed their joy upon the reception of the President's proclamation of freedom, by firing one hundred guns in honor of the event," the newspaper reported, using some odd punctuation, on January 3. "The firing commenced in a late hour in the evening above the Monongahela bridge, and was continued at intervals up to the hour of writing."

"The blow is struck this day which, under the blessing of God, will restore this nation to unity and peace," the *Gazette* opined on its editorial page. The newspaper, a strong supporter of Lincoln, the Republican Party and abolition, sought to tamp down fears that freed blacks either would massacre their former owners in the South or would flood the Northern states, driving down pay for white workers.

"A gentleman with whom we talked yesterday, who has just escaped as a refugee from Georgia, told us that the negroes there all know that they are to be made free on the first of January," the editorial said. "[They] expect

Stained-glass window in Heinz Chapel at the University of Pittsburgh shows Abraham Lincoln and a slave who was freed as a result of the president's Emancipation Proclamation. *Courtesy Darrell Sapp of the* Pittsburgh Post-Gazette.

to remain free where they are and work for wages…This gentleman says the transition from slavery to freedom will not be attended with the smallest danger of disturbance, provided the change be acquiesced in by the masters."

While a majority of Pittsburgh and Allegheny County voters had backed Lincoln and the Republicans in the 1860 election, the city had its share of anti-abolition Democrats.

Pittsburgh Post editor James P. Barr imagined a war of proclamations starting between President Lincoln and Confederate president Jefferson Davis. Both men, he wrote on January 3, were chief executives of their countries and commanders-in-chief of armies. Lincoln's proclamation, citing a wartime emergency and his power as commander-in-chief, freed all slaves in territory in rebellion against the Federal government.

Barr speculated, tongue in cheek, on the Confederate response. "Seven days afterwards, Generalissimo Davis puts forth a vermilion edict," Barr wrote. "I, Jeff Davis…do hereby declare that all negro slaves emancipated by the proclamation of Abraham Lincoln are hereby returned to slavery."

Lincoln then would "rejoin with another ukase, again emancipating the unfortunate victims of Mr. Davis' proclamation." This issuance of rival proclamations would continue until the terms of office ended for each man, Barr wrote.

"Well, now the radicals have got their great panacea; their last desperate move has been made," the *Post* said on January 5. The war began to restore the Union. "Abolitionists have succeeded in diverting the war from its original purpose, to suit themselves, and 'the unalterable rule of right' and 'eternal fitness of things.'"

The *Gazette* agreed that the nature of the conflict had been fundamentally altered by Lincoln's proclamation. "Slaveholders will struggle for a while against the tide that is turned against them," the newspaper concluded. "But they cannot maintain it long; and thus the relation of master to slave will quietly change to that of employer and employee; and those people will prosper best who shall soonest acquiesce in the change."

ALLEGHENY BOYS DON'T LACK WAYS TO FIND TROUBLE

Older readers of the *Daily Pittsburgh Gazette* in the late autumn of 1862 may have wondered what the younger generation was coming to. Even as the

Civil War raged, the newspaper carried stories about teenage tobacco use turning deadly and youth gangs running amok.

Henry McNash, about age sixteen, was "an inveterate tobacco chewer," according to a story in the November 27 edition of the newspaper. The son of a shoemaker, he had been hired as a porter on an Ohio River steamboat that towed barges between Pittsburgh and Cincinnati. He had picked up his nicotine habit on his previous job, "peddling tobacco and cigars."

As his boat reached Marietta, Ohio, "young McNash accidentally fell from the [deck], alighting upon a barge which the steamer had in tow." The drop wasn't far, "but the boy, as usual, had a large quid of tobacco in his mouth, which, by some means or other, he swallowed." Henry was able to climb back onto the steamboat under his own power. "Immediately after getting aboard the boat again, he became very sick and convulsions rapidly followed," according to the story. The boy was seen by a doctor, who could do little. Showing a singular concern about keeping to a schedule, the captain ordered the boat to get under way.

The swallowing incident happened Saturday morning, and for the rest of the day McNash "suffered intensely from spasms." As the steamboat slowly made its way upriver toward Pittsburgh, McNash's convulsions were followed by lethargy and coma. "Animation seemed completely suspended, except when the body was shaken, when slight signs of life were exhibited," the *Gazette* said.

When the steamer reached Pittsburgh Tuesday morning, doctors were called. The first physician predicted McNash would not survive. The teenager rallied later in the day, however, and was able to recognize people, including a second doctor called in on the case.

There was some confusion about the victim's identity that was not solved until the young son of one of the boat's owners recognized him. McNash was carried to the North Side home of his father, in what was then the independent city of Allegheny. The second physician "expressed the opinion that the boy was out of danger, but fully concurred in the opinion...that tobacco was the sole cause of the symptoms."

While Henry was battling to recover from the effects of swallowing too large a wad of tobacco, other Allegheny boys engaged in a rock-throwing battle with youths from across the river. "About two hundred boys were engaged, but no casualties are reported," a December 1 story in the *Gazette* said. "The police pounced down upon them, but the pickets gave the alarm and the 'Allegheny rats' and the 'town rats' (as they are mutually designated) suddenly ceased the combat and fled to their hiding places."

"Only one prisoner was captured, a big hulk of a fellow, old enough to have known better," the newspaper reported. "He was conveyed to the lock-up, where he was enjoying a snooze last night."

Allegheny's mayor, Alexander C. Alexander, was at his wits' end trying to stop the gang fighting, because "boys are harder to catch and more troublesome to deal with than men."

The newspaper warned of tough, if ungrammatical, consequences. The mayor "will resort to harsh measures if the boys does [*sic*] not behave themselves," the *Gazette* reported. "They have become so bad that nothing but sharp punishment will bring them to their senses."

That same edition of the paper provided the sad final chapter to the story of Henry McNash. The sixteen-year-old never recovered from what the *Gazette* described as "a death-like lethargy" following his ingestion of tobacco. He died on November 29.

CITY DIGS IN AS LEE INVADES THE NORTH

Pittsburgh offered a tempting target for Confederate forces, Abraham Lincoln told a visitor to his office on June 18, 1863. "The President talked a good deal about Pittsburgh," a "gentleman of this city" wrote in a letter from Washington published June 22 in the *Daily Pittsburgh Gazette*. Such private correspondence was often the source of out-of-town stories for the region's newspapers.

According to Lincoln, Pittsburgh "was more an object [of military importance] both to the rebels and the country than Harrisburg, as there was an arsenal, some gun foundries, and a good deal of boat building." Lincoln's comments added to the multiple reports that identified the Forks of the Ohio as a possible target when General Robert E. Lee's Army of Northern Virginia invaded Pennsylvania in June 1863. Of even greater concern was the whereabouts of Confederate general J.E.B. Stuart's fast-moving cavalry. No one knew where Stuart's horsemen would turn up next.

A New York businessman named Hewitt had arrived in the city after a journey to Vicksburg. "He informed one of our leading merchants that it had long been the intention of the rebels to destroy Pittsburgh," according to a *Gazette* story that appeared on June 5. "He wished our citizens to be on their guard." Another Pittsburgher told of a conversation with a Rebel officer, "in which he stated that it was their intention to destroy the cannon

Nobody knew where Confederate general Robert E. Lee and his army were when they invaded Pennsylvania in June 1863. Image from *Harper's Pictorial History of the Civil War Part First. Courtesy Senator John Heinz History Center.*

foundry as soon as it was possible for them to do so." That reference was to the Fort Pitt Foundry, located in what is now Pittsburgh's Strip District, where heavy artillery was produced.

Pittsburgh and its sister city of Allegheny were rail hubs and home to hundreds of factories and warehouses. The Federal government's Allegheny Arsenal was only a few miles away in what was then the separate borough of Lawrenceville.

During that first week in June, residents formed committees of public safety to defend their communities. "The best mode for preventing attack is to be at all times thoroughly prepared for our defense," committee members said in a statement published on June 6. Less than a week later, General William T.H. Brooks arrived in Pittsburgh to organize the military and civilian defense of the region as commander of the Department of the Monongahela. Brooks asked that business and factory owners provide at least two thousand men to start digging entrenchments to protect approaches to Allegheny and Pittsburgh. Meeting on June 14 at the Monongahela House on Smithfield Street, the community leaders agreed.

The *Gazette* on June 15 contained some slightly reassuring news. Lee's army had been located on the eastern side of the Allegheny Mountains near Winchester, Virginia, and Martinsburg, in the new breakaway state of West Virginia. That made a Confederate attack on Harrisburg or Philadelphia more likely than a move against Pittsburgh. But the location of Stuart's cavalry remained unknown. The public safety committee asked, in a story that appeared on June 17, that Allegheny County men "capable of bearing arms forthwith enroll themselves in military organizations for drill, active service and defensive warfare." All others were asked to "form themselves into squads for labor, and work upon the fortifications for defense and security of this vicinity."

By the end of that week almost 4,500 men were digging trenches and putting up earthworks on high ground around the cities. The *Gazette* on June 19 ran lists of companies and the number of workers they provided for defense. Iron makers Jones and Laughlin, for example, had 350 of its workers laboring on Mount Washington.

The *Gazette* reported that same day that the city's black residents were eager to do their part to defend their homes. "We are informed that the colored men of the two cities sent a deputation to the military authorities, tending their services in any capacity," the story said. Almost six months after the Emancipation Proclamation freed all slaves in secessionist states, the issue of using black volunteers remained controversial. General Brooks did not reply to the proposal from the African American community to provide about two hundred men.

"The offer, however was honorable to them, and we hope that matters can yet be so arranged that they may have an opportunity to render their assistance," the newspaper said. The story noted that some blacks were already at work. "We knew that a band of colored men were engaged on the works on the south side of the Monongahela, and are informed that they labored with great energy."

The *Gazette* also warned that Pittsburgh was in danger of falling behind its cross-state rival in its racial attitudes: "In Philadelphia the services of two or three companies of colored men were offered and accepted, as we see by the papers of that city."

In that same day's paper, a familiar name turns up. Joseph Horne, who founded a famous department store that bore his family name, proposed at a public safety meeting that the merchants of Pittsburgh "suspend all business until the present emergency has passed." His motion was approved. By June 20 more than 6,800 workers were digging fortifications on Mount Washington, Squirrel Hill and more than two dozen other locations around the two cities.

Not everyone was following the rules. The *Gazette* reported on June 25 that a gang of men had walked down what was then Liberty Street "for the purpose of compelling certain shop keepers to close up their stores." Most complied, the story said.

One exception was M. Amburgh, a clothier at the corner of Liberty and Smithfield Streets. Although his salesman, H.S. Solomons, urged him to close, Amburgh "became very indignant [and] declared he would not shut his store." When Solomons refused to fetch police to disperse the crowd of protestors, Amburgh fired him. He then briefly closed his store, "but after the crowd left, he opened the front door."

Conditions grew tenser as the Confederates occupied more Pennsylvania towns. *Gazette* headlines on June 25 told of "15,000 Rebels in the Cumberland Valley" and "Chambersburg Taken and Gutted." On June 29, Pittsburgh readers learned that "Carlisle [was] evacuated by our troops" and "Longstreet and Ewell's Corps in Pennsylvania."

Work on fortifications around the city continued into the first days of July with a goal of completing them by Independence Day. General Brooks had ordered bars and saloons to close on Friday and Saturday, July 3 and 4. His proclamation, published in the July 3 *Gazette*, banned both "the selling or giving away" of alcohol. "The carrying of beer, ale or any kind of liquor to the working parties also is forbidden."

"The Fourth passed off very quietly and pleasantly in this vicinity," the *Gazette* reported on Monday, July 6. "There was a very general response to the call to work upon the fortifications, and thousands were thus employed...the number of ladies who visited the earth works during the day was very large."

While work on all the fortifications had not been completed by the July 4 deadline, the urgency dissipated. What the *Gazette* called the "Great Battle near Gettysburg" had ended with Lee's army retreating south. The big danger to Pennsylvania had passed.

Union and Confederate forces clashed in the biggest battle of the Civil War at Gettysburg in July 1863. Image from *Harper's Pictorial History of the Civil War Part Second. Courtesy Senator John Heinz History Center.*

As it wound down its affairs, the public safety committee on July 7 passed a resolution to halt all paid labor on the redoubts, forts and trenches. Members also offered a tribute to those who labored on the defenses: "Whereas, during the last three weeks many skilled workmen and mechanics, suspending their usual avocations, have devoted their time and labor to the construction of the fortifications around the city…this committee acknowledges the services of these patriotic fellow citizens who have thus nobly sacrificed their individual advantage for the public benefit."

PITTSBURGH'S SANITARY FAIR PROVES BETTER THAN AVERAGE

Although he had spent many years working as a corporate lawyer, Abraham Lincoln was known to many as the "rail splitter." The nickname was a reference to his humble origins and his work as a young man, turning logs into fence rails.

Visitors to the Pittsburgh Sanitary Fair, a regional fundraising effort to benefit wounded and sick Union soldiers, would get a chance to see one of the rails that Lincoln made during his early days. The wooden artifact was one of more than one thousand items to be displayed in the fair's "Old Curiosity Shop," according to an advance story in the May 13, 1864 edition of the *Daily Pittsburgh Gazette*.

The fair would open June 1 on the Diamond in Allegheny City. Displays would occupy five temporary buildings and the Allegheny City Hall, near Federal and Ohio Streets. A seventh building, a temporary auditorium called the "audience hall," had room for more than three thousand spectators.

Standard admission to the fair's Floral or Dining Halls was fifty cents, equivalent to more than seven dollars in modern currency. Entry to other structures, including the Ladies' Bazaar, Mechanics' Hall, Picture Gallery and Monitor Building, cost twenty-five cents each.

The display planned for the Monitor Building was designed to provide visitors an "idea of naval warfare on a small scale." Craftsmen from the Fort Pitt Iron Works, which made armor plate for the U.S. government, were building a nine-foot-long model of a Union navy ironclad ship for display at the fair. The vessel would steam around a forty- by fifty-foot indoor pond. "She will be fitted up with an engine…and the gun will be so arranged that it can be fired off," a May 6 story in the *Gazette* explained.

Weather cooperated for the opening day of the fair. "Providence seemed to smile upon the noble efforts made in behalf of the sick and disabled soldiers," the *Gazette* said on June 2. "The request of the Mayors of both cities for a suspension of business was cordially acceded to—workshops, stores, factories,

Pittsburgh's 1864 Sanitary Fair raised about $300,000 for sick and wounded soldiers. *Courtesy Senator John Heinz History Center.*

schools and even private dwellings were abandoned and the people turned out en masse to witness the procession and attend the inauguration ceremonies."

Governor Andrew Curtin was the main speaker at the opening. Knowing that there were events like the Sanitary Fair happening in Pittsburgh and other major cities offered hope and comfort to soldiers in the field, he said. "It is important that each soldier knows that those who are at home are preparing, constantly preparing, the means which are to provide for him, whether sick or wounded," the governor said. And if he died, "those near and dear to him are to be kindly and liberally cared for."

Paintings, machinery, floral arrangements, autographed books and historical artifacts were displayed for purchase or viewing in the fair buildings. Food in the Dining Hall would be prepared on an "extensive cooking range…upon which will be fried, stewed, baked, roasted, boiled and broiled everything that can gratify the tastes of the daintiest epicure or most voracious gourmand." Lighter refreshments in the Floral Hall included fresh fruit, ice cream and what the newspaper called "soda," rather than "pop."

Patrons of Pittsburgh's Sanitary Fair included many of the region's most prominent residents. *Courtesy Senator John Heinz History Center.*

Business owners and individuals had been asked to make cash contributions before the fair opened. Organizers reported that $100,000—equivalent to more than $1.4 million in modern currency—had been collected by opening day. That early result offered hope that the event might raise as much as $250,000 by its conclusion on June 18.

The Audience Hall, also referred to in advertisements as the Grand Concert Hall, drew a variety of performers. They included the Hyatt Cadets, a 170-member military drill team, and gymnasts, in full costume, who performed "a series of feats with the light dumb-bells, the gymnastic rings, wands and the Indian clubs."

A singing group still well known in Pittsburgh performed on June 6. The Teutonia Maennerchor, which maintains its headquarters on Pittsburgh's North Side, took part in a performance by four combined choirs and three orchestras. The work was called "On the Seashore," or in German, *"Am Meeres Strande."*

The June 10 edition of the *Gazette* provided a reminder of why the fair was important. A *Gazette* correspondent, writing under the name "Nemo," gave the names and injuries of fourteen Pittsburgh soldiers wounded during recent battles in Virginia. Those on Nemo's list included R.G. Thomas, hit in the right leg; Horatio Goldthorp, a slight head wound; Lieutenant James McIntire, hurt in the right arm; and James McKee, who died "in an ambulance at White House Landing."

"There are about two thousand wounded men here. They are being attended to as well as could be expected," Nemo reported. "Our Western Pennsylvania soldiers learned with inexpressible delight and exultant pride that the Pittsburgh Sanitary Fair opened successfully," he wrote.

Pittsburgh residents were proving to be generous. By June 13, fair activities already had raised $257,000, according to the newspaper. Ultimately the fair raised $300,000 by the time it closed, with proceeds from an estimated $30,000 in unsold merchandise yet to be added to the total. Those numbers were in a June 20 wrap-up story in the *Gazette*.

One of the good works begun at the Sanitary Fair continues into the twenty-first century. When the Civil War effectively ended with Robert E. Lee's surrender on April 9, 1865, about $200,000 remained unspent from the profits of the fair. According to historian Leland D. Baldwin, that money became the "nucleus" of the endowment fund for Western Pennsylvania Hospital, now part of West Penn Allegheny Health System.

REAL MATH TRUMPS DEMOCRATS' OPTIMISM

As more states on the electoral map turned blue on election night 2012, indicating victory for President Barack Obama, Fox News anchor Megyn Kelly famously questioned analyst Karl Rove about the nature of his voter projections. "Is this just math that you do as a Republican to make yourself feel better, or is this real?" she asked him.

GEORGE B. McCLELLAN.

George McClellan left the Union army to run against Abraham Lincoln in 1864. Image from *Harper's Pictorial History of the Civil War Part First. Courtesy Senator John Heinz History Center.*

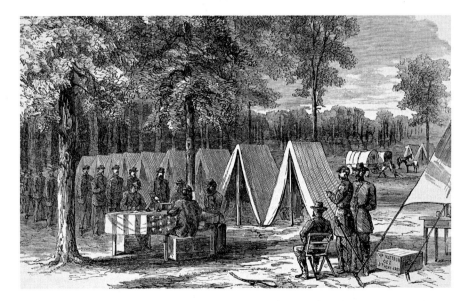

Soldiers were able to vote in the field during the election of 1864. Image from *Harper's Pictorial History of the Civil War Part Second. Courtesy Senator John Heinz History Center.*

A similar question might have been put to James P. Barr in November 1864. He was the editor of the *Pittsburgh Post*, the city's Democratic-leaning newspaper. Despite worrisome results in congressional elections a month earlier that showed Republican gains, Democrats in southwestern Pennsylvania were counting on a win in the presidential contest. Six days before the election, "the Democracy of Washington, Beaver and Allegheny counties, with their wives, children and sweethearts, turned out en masse to vindicate the Union and the Constitution," the *Post* reported on November 4. The mass meeting was held in Clinton, Findlay Township.

The march of Democratic supporters, led by Allegheny County delegations from Moon, Crescent, North Fayette and Findlay, "took three quarters of an hour to pass," the newspaper said. "The States were represented by a wagon filled with young girls, appropriately clad and adorned, drawn by 35 horses ridden by lads uniformly clothed."

Why thirty-five horses and riders? The Union, until the admission of Nevada on October 31, 1864, had thirty-five states.

"The regalia, transparencies, enthusiasm and display generally far exceeded anything ever before seen in that vicinity," the *Post* concluded. "The whole affair was a triumphant success and will do good service for the Union and McClellan."

Union general George McClellan had resigned from the army to run as the Democratic Party candidate against Abraham Lincoln. Lincoln, a Republican, and his vice-presidential running mate, Andrew Johnson, a Democratic senator from secessionist Tennessee, ran as National Union Party candidates.

Just as Lincoln had persuaded a Democrat to run with him, Pittsburgh's Democracy—as the party referred to itself—found a former Republican to back McClellan. "The last grand rally of the Democracy of Lawrenceville will be held on Saturday evening next, at the corner of Butler and Allen streets," the *Post* reported on November 4. Speakers would include Thomas Little, described as "the facetious captain of the 1860 Lincoln Ox Roast…and a former leader of the Lawrenceville Wide-Awakes." It had taken him four years, but Little was "now thoroughly awakened" to the dangers posed by Lincoln and the Republicans, the newspaper said. (The "Wide-Awakes" were young men's political clubs organized to support the Republican Party. Carrying oil lamps or torches in nighttime parades, members had provided security at campaign rallies and carried out some quasi-military drilling.)

Lincoln was counting on votes from soldiers as one of the keys to his reelection, but the *Post* ran several stories suggesting he would have trouble on that front. "The vote of the Army is for Little Mac," the newspaper reported on November 3, reprinting a letter that had appeared in the *New York World.* "My regiment voted today," the letter said. The newspaper identified the writer as an officer with the New York Eighty-eighth Infantry Regiment. The reported unanimous result, however, would not have seemed out of place in a North Korean election. "There were two hundred entitled to vote, and they all voted for McClellan and [New York governor Horatio] Seymour," the officer claimed. He and his comrades were lucky to be able to vote: "You know most of the soldiers who served under McClellan are dead, while most of the fellows who are now voting for Lincoln were at home at ease."

Pittsburgh Republicans appeared unfazed by Democratic attacks. The pages of the *Daily Pittsburgh Gazette,* the city's Republican newspaper, contained multiple advertisements for GOP rallies around the region. German-speaking voters were invited in that day's paper to a November 5 mass meeting at Pittsburgh's Concert Hall on Wood Street. There, Fredrick Hauserick, a politician from Cincinnati, would address them in their native language. A "Grand Union Mass Convention" was scheduled for noon that same day in Elizabeth Borough. "Union men of Pittsburgh and vicinity" were instructed to assemble that morning at Wilkins Hall, on what is now Fourth Avenue, at "7½ o'clock and proceed to the Brownsville Wharf." There "a special steamer, chartered for the occasion, will convey the delegation to Elizabeth Borough. A Brass Band will be in attendance."

Not to be outdone by the Democrats in rural areas, the Republicans held their own tri-county rally in Findlay at noon on November 5: "The unfavorable weather did not prevent the sturdy yeomen from turning out in company with their families, and giving a day to the cause of Lincoln and Liberty."

If the Democrats claimed their parade was three-quarters of a mile long, the GOP "procession was over a mile in length." Like the "Democracy" the previous week, the Republicans mounted pretty girls on horses. "Each lady wore a blue sash on which was inscribed, on a white ground in black letters, the name of the state which she represented. The seceded states were represented by eleven ladies on horseback, in mourning, and carrying a small banner, on one side of which was the inscription—Our Folly makes us Mourn."

On election day, both papers warned voters to look out for fraud. "The one especial need today is vigilance," the *Gazette* said. "The polls must be closely watched."

"If any Democrat shall tender his vote [and] the election officers should refuse to receive it, let him not rest here," the *Post* advised. "Let him take two or three witnesses and demand that he shall deposit his ballot."

Reporting on the election itself, the *Gazette* on November 9 grew poetic in describing the balloting: "All is moving on as quietly as the fall of a calm snow shower. Each citizen walks up, deposits his little ballot and retires. What one man does seems to be a little thing in itself…and it is only when we take in the sum total of these things—that the sublimity and grandeur of the thing strikes home upon the mind."

The *Post* agreed that the election "passed off quietly enough so far as we have heard." The exception was one ward in Allegheny City "where the Abolitionists, early after the polls were opened, manifested a disposition to carry matters in a high hand; but the firm stand taken by the Democrats deterred them from carrying out their designs."

The next-day results, however, were not looking good for McClellan. "Abolitionists appear to have increased their majority by a few hundred since the last election. The aggregate vote is astonishingly large…which can be accounted for in no way except by illegal voting," the *Post* said. By Thursday morning, November 10, the *Post* could not avoid doing real math: "Although we concede the election of Mr. Lincoln, the result will show that he escaped defeat very narrowly."

The *Gazette* was jubilant. "It is impossible to overestimate the importance of Tuesday's vote," the newspaper said that same day. "It is an emphatic declaration of the people that this war shall be vigorously prosecuted to the complete suppression of the rebellion…from the result of this election, this glorious civil victory, achieved as it was in the face of a powerful armed foe in the field, and in the midst of multitudinous conspirators, we may assuredly infer that God is with us."

Lincoln and Johnson had racked up a 45 to 55 percent victory in the popular vote and an overwhelming win in the electoral college. McClellan carried only Delaware, Kentucky and New Jersey.

By turning out to vote, Pittsburgh and Allegheny County residents had played an important part in that triumph. The city's contribution was recognized in a poem written by a Philadelphia lawyer named James Graham and published on November 9 in the *Gazette*:

> *Hurrah, you dwellers in the smoke,*
> *The neck of Little Mac is broke;*
> *The loyal city of old Penn*
> *Again rolls up her thousands ten.*
> *The Union's safe, and freedom too,*
> *Says Yankee doodle, doodle doo.*

Chapter 5

News from the Battlefield

REUNION AT FORTRESS MONROE

In the months after Northern soldiers had been routed at the First Battle of Bull Run in July 1861, it became clear that the War of Southern Rebellion would not be over by Christmas. Supporters of the Union, however, could take comfort in knowing that the Stars and Stripes continued to fly over Fortress Monroe, eighty miles southeast of Richmond, even after Virginia seceded in May 1861.

In October 1861, a correspondent for the *Daily Pittsburgh Gazette* filed a report from what was the only U.S. military installation on the Virginia Peninsula not to have been occupied by Confederate forces. Union navy ships were there in force, according to the "Letter from Fortress Monroe" published on October 26. The author was identified only by the initial "R." As many as forty military vessels had assembled, he reported. They were part of a blockade force designed to strangle the Confederacy by cutting off its trade with Europe. "Some are propellers and some are side-wheel steamers; but all are fast sailers, and all able to protect themselves," according to the story.

Fortress Monroe was important for another reason. It served as a refuge for fleeing Virginia slaves. The fort's commander, General Benjamin Butler, had announced in May that slaves who reached the fort would be considered "contraband," and Federal forces would not return them to their owners. By September, the United States was paying and providing daily rations for those who had escaped in return for their labor. Fortress Monroe became the

Pittsburgh residents made visits to Fortress Monroe, Virginia, which remained in Union hands during the Civil War. Image from *Harper's Pictorial History of the Civil War Part First. Courtesy Senator John Heinz History Center.*

Slaves freed themselves even before the Emancipation Proclamation by seeking protection at Fortress Monroe. Image from *Harper's Pictorial History of the Civil War Part First. Courtesy Senator John Heinz History Center.*

first of many "contraband camps" that housed men, women and children seeking freedom.

Point Comfort, on which the military camp had been built, had been "a favorite summer resort for sea bathing," *Gazette* readers learned. When war came, the U.S. government had taken over the lone hotel there and converted most of it into a hospital. "The fortress, the government offices and warehouses and the hotel constitute all the buildings to be seen," the *Gazette* correspondent wrote. "The 'contraband' are quartered in the oldest and most tumble-down of the government houses."

The reporter found little to interest him. "When you have 'done' the fortress, looked at the Union guns, chatted with the 'contraband,' taken a gaze at [Confederate-controlled] Sewell's Point…and a stroll over a fine gravel road to the ruins of Hampton, you have seen all that is to be seen."

The anonymous "R" was not the only Pittsburgh reporter to have traveled to Fortress Monroe. Another *Gazette* correspondent, identified by the initial "C," described his experience "during a recent visit" to the camp's hotel-turned-hospital. His story appeared December 2. His companions included Pittsburgh resident Mary Moorhead, "the amiable and accomplished daughter of the Hon. J.K. Moorhead," a businessman and member of Congress. During her visit to the hospital, she stopped "at the couch of a fine looking Indiana soldier" to offer "a word of comfort and of hope amidst fevers, pains and sorrows."

The wounded soldier told the woman, "'I think I know you.' To her reply, 'How can you possibly know me?' he very feelingly rejoined, 'I remember you gave me my supper at Pittsburgh.'" Union troops traveling through the city traditionally were fed by a "Subsistence Committee," in which young female volunteers served.

"Is there not in this incident much to encourage our ladies to continue in well doing?" the reporter asked. "Miss Mary," he wrote, should "not be the only person to enjoy personally the grateful remembrance of a wounded soldier."

PITTSBURGH'S NEGLEY TRIES TOUGH LOVE IN TENNESSEE

About five hundred people around Columbia, Tennessee, took an oath of allegiance to the United States in the summer of 1862.

The number of residents reaffirming their support for the Federal government was equal to the number of Union soldiers occupying the region,

Pittsburgh general James Negley said secessionists were much worse than thieves. Image from *Harper's Pictorial History of the Civil War Part Second.* Courtesy Senator John Heinz History Center.

according to an August 9 story in the *Daily Pittsburgh Gazette.* Those troops were under the command of General James S. Negley, an Allegheny County native who began his military experience as a private during the Mexican-American War. Pittsburgh's Negley Avenue is named for him.

He was left in charge when his superior, Don Carlos Buell, withdrew the bulk of Union force from the region. Negley "was complete master of all the roads in Middle Tennessee," according to the *Gazette* story. His troops controlled several of the area's principal railroads and supply routes and protected them from damage: "No bridges were destroyed and but a few minor depredations were committed."

Negley sought to get Tennesseans to affirm their loyalty to the Federal government. In a "stringent oath," they swore to "maintain the national sovereignty paramount to that of all State, county, or corporate powers" and to "discourage, discountenance and forever oppose secession, rebellion, or disintegration of the Federal Union…and disclaim and denounce all faith and fellowship with the so-called Confederate states." The penalty for the "violation of this oath is death."

While Union armies saw success in Tennessee, troops under General George McClellan failed in attempts to take the Confederate capital of Richmond, Virginia. Those defeats in the Peninsula Campaign had "occasioned a tumultuous flutter among the rebels" in Tennessee, according to the paper. When a former senator named Alfred Osborn Pope Nicholson joined the celebrations, Negley ordered him arrested. Nicholson, who had a long career in state politics and journalism, had served two periods in the U.S. Senate, leaving in March 1861, just before Tennessee seceded. Negley ordered that Nicholson be kept "in close confinement, on soldier's fare" as "an avowed traitor to his country."

The ex-senator retained plenty of friends, according to the *Gazette*, and some pressured Negley to release him. The general "informed them all that he would transgress his duty should he release so vile a traitor."

Even the pleas of Nicholson's feisty wife did not change Negley's mind. On the day of his arrest, she asked if she could take her husband a pillow and some food. The general refused. She then asked where her husband was being held. "In the guard house, Madame, with a soldier who has been imprisoned for stealing," she was told. "This enraged the lady and she inquired of the officer if he meant to compare the crime of her husband to the petty transgressions of a low blackguard of a soldier."

Negley said it was the thief who should be offended, because Nicholson's offense was much worse. "[You] must not consider me indelicate when I inform you that your husband deserves hanging," he told her. "Mrs. Nicholson immediately bestowed upon the General the vilest of abuse, and exhausted the vocabulary of opprobrious epithets in her rage." Nicholson escaped hanging, and his time in jail for loyalty to what Southerners referred to as "The Lost Cause" did him no long-term harm. He went on to serve as chief justice of the Tennessee Supreme Court from 1870 until his death six years later.

Negley, too, had political success. He returned to Pittsburgh after the war and represented the region for several terms in Congress. He is buried in Allegheny Cemetery in Pittsburgh's Lawrenceville neighborhood.

REVENGE FOR BULL RUN AT SOUTH MOUNTAIN

Charles William Owston joined the Pittsburgh Rifles in April 1861 as a private. By August 1862, he was captain of what had become Company A of the Ninth Pennsylvania Reserves. That placed him in the front lines when his unit battled entrenched Confederates guarding Maryland mountain passes at the Battle of South Mountain.

The Pennsylvania Reserves marched more than fifteen miles on Sunday, September 14. It was about 3:00 p.m. when they formed their battle line. "The enemy were posted upon the heights in front of [Union] Gen. Hooker's Corps...and the task before our brave boys was to dislodge them," a writer identified only as C.W.S. wrote in a letter printed on September

20 in the *Daily Pittsburgh Gazette.* Letters from what would now be called "citizen journalists" were a common source of news from military camps and battlefields. C.W.S. explained that he was writing on behalf of Captain Owston, who had been wounded in the hand during the battle.

The Ninth Pennsylvania had been waiting for another chance to face the enemy ever since the Union defeat at Bull Run, "when under the leadership of Gens. [Irvin] McDowell and [John] Pope, they had been beaten and forced to fall back."

"[They] had longed for this hour, when under the direction of their own leader, Gen. [George B.] McClellan, the order might be given to 'charge.'

"They advanced in the face of the enemy's fire, losing in the charge many noble men," the letter said. "But nothing daunted, upward they moved, firing as they went...when, with a wild shout of victory, they rushed upon them with the bayonets."

The Confederates withdrew, "moving off in confusion, from a position which a few hours before they had seemed determined to maintain." The Ninth Pennsylvania took many prisoners, "and here at least felt that the long weary day of marching and fighting had not been in vain...and the hitherto proud and defiant enemy were compelled...to flee before our advancing columns."

The cost had been heavy. "But ah! there are incidents connected with every victory which serve to temper our joy," C.W.S. wrote. "The world will never know how many bitter tears have been shed over these sad victories."

"John Copley fell early in the engagement, mortally wounded, and lingered till next morning," the writer reported. "His friends have the consolation of knowing that kind friends ministered to him in the hour of death, and sadly and sorrowfully prepared him for his burial." Copley was the son of a *Gazette* editor, Josiah Copley Sr.

The *Gazette* had a follow-up story on September 22, telling readers that Captain Owston was on the mend. "His wound is in the third finger of the right hand—painful and troublesome, but not at all dangerous," the correspondent said.

Maryland families in Middletown and Frederick were taking good care of Union casualties. "Capt. Owston says that the kindness of the people of Maryland surpassed anything he ever saw," according to the story. "Every house was made a hospital, every man, woman and child was a physician and nurse."

While the Union armies were able to clear the mountain passes, most military historians fault McClellan for not following up quickly on the day's win, giving Confederate commander Robert E. Lee a chance to concentrate his forces for a much larger battle. That fight would take place a few days later near the banks of Antietam Creek.

PITTSBURGH RIFLES IN THE FRONT LINES AT ANTIETAM

When Union and Confederate troops collided in a cornfield near Antietam Creek 150 years ago, soldiers from the Pennsylvania Reserves were in the front lines.

Volunteers from an Allegheny County unit, known as the Pittsburgh Rifles, were in a crucial position during the battle near Sharpsburg, Maryland, according to a report in the September 26, 1862 edition of the *Daily Pittsburgh Gazette*. When General Joseph Hooker led almost nine thousand men against the Confederates before dawn on September 17, the Pennsylvania Reserves' Ninth Regiment anchored the right flank of the Union line. The men of the Pittsburgh Rifles—Company A of the Ninth Regiment—were, in turn, the far end of the Union line. It was "a position of great danger and importance, and one which was well sustained, never yielding for a moment before that dreadful sheet of fire," the anonymous correspondent for the *Gazette* wrote.

The two armies were about twenty-five yards apart when the battle opened with point-blank firing. "A perfect sheet of flame seemed to issue from our ranks, but although the rebels fell by hundreds, their front remained unbroken and their fire unslackened." Musket balls filled "the air in a perfect storm…described by an eyewitness as having the appearance of a handful of beans flung right into their faces.

The Battle of Antietam was the bloodiest single day in U.S. history, and the morning's fight was the most costly. Historians estimate casualties at one per second during the first few hours.

While Union forces were able temporarily to drive "the butternuts back, back, through the corn, through the adjoining open field," the Confederates soon regrouped and counterattacked, regaining most of the ground they had lost. The *Gazette* reporter called the Southerners "butternuts" because many were wearing tan uniforms that recalled the color of butternut squash.

Following the morning's fight for the cornfield, the battle shifted south to areas now known as "Bloody Lane" and "Burnside Bridge." By evening, neither army had won a clear victory, but neither had retreated. About

The stone bridge across Antietam Creek was the scene of some of the heaviest fighting in the single-bloodiest day of the Civil War. Image from *Harper's Pictorial History of the Civil War Part Second*. *Courtesy Senator John Heinz History Center.*

twenty-three thousand men were dead, wounded or missing in what appeared to be a stalemate.

The next day was "a day of rest—such rest as can be found with three miles of dead men to bury, and thousands of wounded to bring from the field," according to "letters from the battle-field" published on September 24 in the *Gazette*. While generals could not agree on terms for a cease-fire, "by common consent, both the rebels and our own soldiers were mingling freely, taking away the wounded."

While both sides allowed casualties to be carried from the field, Confederate snipers sought to punish any Union efforts to gather intelligence. "Whenever the enemy detected anyone using a field glass on his camp or battery, his sharpshooters would at once reopen [firing], notwithstanding the informal truce."

Union commander George McClellan appeared satisfied with the battlefield results when Confederate general Robert E. Lee withdrew across the Potomac back into Virginia on the night of September 18–19. "Maryland and Pennsylvania are now safe," he wrote in a famous dispatch. Like President Lincoln, however, the editor of the *Gazette* was disappointed with the result. On September 20, the newspaper said a real defeat for the Rebels would have meant trapping the Confederates at the rain-swollen river, forcing them "to lay down their arms and surrender or be annihilated."

UNION PAYS FOR DELAY AT FREDERICKSBURG

Major General Ambrose Burnside moved fast in mid-November 1862. He assembled a Union army of more than 100,000 men on the north shore of the Rappahannock River, but he found himself blocked by logistics. The pontoon bridges he needed to cross the broad, cold river and open the way to Richmond, Virginia, were not there when the first units of his Army of the Potomac arrived on November 17.

Northern newspapers had been expecting a climactic battle, but days turned into weeks with little action other than occasional artillery duels. "From one of the bluffs of the Rappahannock, we had a fine view of Fredericksburg," a *Daily Pittsburgh Gazette* story said on November 24. The Yankee observer wrote that he could see "two long trains of [railroad] cars, just starting toward Richmond, conveying away the last 'portable property' of the Rebel troops...they evidently did not mean to make a strong stand against us; but careful scrutiny with field glasses showed four of their guns in position, ready to detain us as long as possible." Two batteries from the First New York Artillery came forward, "planted on a commanding hill...just as they were fairly in position, the rebels opened with their 10-pound Parrotts, at a distance of 1,600 yards, with the river between us."

The *Gazette* account stated that the Confederate guns "over-shot, and their fuses were a trifle too long."

"One of their shells knocked a spoke from the wheel of one of our caissons, but the others all passed over our heads, and we had no casualties whatever," the account continued. The Union guns, however, "made it so hot for them that they all ran away into the woods...they afterward ventured out, and by great activity, succeeded in withdrawing their guns to the protection of the forest, where they finally disappeared."

Artillery success was overshadowed by Southern activity on the other side of the river while the Union forces waited for their temporary bridges. "Availing themselves of the opportunity so unexpectedly afforded them by our delay, the rebels are exerting themselves to the utmost in the erection of earthworks and batteries, new ones appearing almost daily," according to a November 29 story.

Meanwhile, one property owner in Fredericksburg and many local farmers were trying an imaginative approach to protect their property. "A British flag is displayed on one of the houses in the city," the *Gazette* story said. "Many of the citizens hereabouts claim to be British subjects," using that assertion "as a safeguard against the seizure of forage and the occupancy of their premises by military authorities."

As November turned into December with no action, rumors spread that the invasion across the Rappahannock would be delayed until spring. The reason for the stalemate along the banks of the river was described in print in convoluted language that would make any present-day Department of Defense spokesperson envious: "The present delay is owing to certain changes in the situation, which is only to take such steps as will insure the vigorous and successful prosecution of the campaign when reopened."

When the Union effort to cross the Rappahannock "reopened" on December 11, General Burnside assured his superiors in Washington that he had enough troops to attack the entrenched Confederate armies.

"Lincoln and [army general-in-chief Henry] Halleck both seem to feel quite easy, which is interpreted as meaning that they know of something outside of the situation at Fredericksburg to render the position more perfectly satisfactory than it yet seems to the public," the *Gazette* reported on December 15. "Burnside...does not ask for any more men. He says he has all he can use."

Optimism diminished over the next few days, however, as battlefield reports made clear the size of Union losses following the long-delayed Union frontal attack. Burnside's bold but botched plan to cross the Rappahannock River, take Fredericksburg and then capture nearby Richmond ended with a Northern retreat.

On December 18, the *Gazette* carried what it described as an eyewitness report on the battle. The writer described multiple advances on the breastworks and rifle pits that the Confederates, commanded by Robert E. Lee, had built on the hills outside Fredericksburg.

The Army of the Potomac's Second Division, commanded by General John Gibbon, had momentary success in dislodging Lee's troops. "They pushed determinedly through the brushwood and bushes on to a grove of cedars, and through these up the hills towards the breastworks of the enemy. The works were carried, many prisoners captured and the crest of the hill gained, not, however, without heavy loss." Gibbon was among the wounded, hit in the arm while leading the attack.

The Confederates soon brought in reinforcements, and the Union soldiers were forced to retreat.

General Ambrose Burnside had enough men but not enough pontoon bridges when he needed them. Image from *Harper's Pictorial History of the Civil War Part Second. Courtesy Senator John Heinz History Center.*

When Union forces finally crossed the Rappahannock River at Fredericksburg, they found the Confederates dug in on high ground above the town. Image from *Harper's Pictorial History of the Civil War Part Second. Courtesy Senator John Heinz History Center.*

Elsewhere on the battlefield, troops under General Abner Doubleday pushed the Confederates back a mile to their defensive lines, where the Union attack stalled under artillery fire: "During three successive advances and checks...uninterrupted shelling was kept up by rebel batteries upon the bodies of [Union] troops at different points of the plain."

With the early winter darkness, firing slowed around 5:30 p.m. and ceased by 6:00 p.m. "On the left as well as on the right the battle came short of our expectations," the *Gazette*'s on-the-scene observer wrote. "We gained some ground, but failed to realize the main object of the day's work—namely the dislodgment of the enemy from their entrenched position on the heights overlooking the plain."

Initial orders called for renewed attacks the next day, but Burnside ultimately was talked out of making another assault, and the Union army withdrew across the Rappahannock on December 15.

"The position of the enemy at Fredericksburg was found to be too strong to be carried," the *Gazette* concluded, describing the event as "a repulse, not a defeat." The rival *Pittsburgh Post* was less charitable, calling the Union assaults on heavily fortified positions "a shocking blunder and disaster."

The *Post* predicted that Burnside would be sacked and that Lincoln would recall General McClellan to command the Army of the Potomac. The *Gazette* scoffed, but its rival was proved half right. Burnside soon was replaced, but by General "Fighting Joe" Hooker, not McClellan.

After orchestrating the slaughter at Fredericksburg, General Lee mused aloud about the brutal nature of armed conflict: "It is well that war is so terrible—otherwise we would grow too fond of it."

A POW TOURS THE SOUTH

Pittsburgh resident Josiah Copley Jr. saw more of the Confederacy than he wished to.

Josiah, a member of the Twenty-first Illinois Infantry, and his older brother, Albert, a member of the Seventy-eighth Pennsylvania Infantry, were captured separately at the Battle of Stones River, Tennessee, on December 31, 1862. Both were put on trains filled with prisoners that were routed and rerouted all over the South.

Albert, however, had been wounded by an exploding shell and was removed from his train at Knoxville, where he died. "He sleeps in an unmarked grave," according to a 1914 history of Armstrong County.

Josiah ultimately was transported back North and confined in Richmond's Libby Prison. He was exchanged after spending three weeks in a jail that he described as being "in a most filthy condition, and swarming with vermin."

The two brothers were the sons of Pittsburgh newspaper editor Josiah Copley. No sooner had Josiah Jr. been freed from the Confederate prison than he wrote a two-part report for the *Daily Pittsburgh Gazette* on his journey. He described what he had observed as he was transported for two thousand miles through the rebellious South.

About eight hundred Union prisoners were crowded into freight and cattle cars—as many as seventy men to a car—for a journey that carried them through Chattanooga and Atlanta. "We made a slow progress, not over eight miles an hour," he wrote in a story that appeared on February 14, 1863. "Although raining most of the time, I preferred riding on top, to being crowded in the cars, besides it afforded a better chance of seeing the country."

Whenever the train stopped on the journey through the Deep South, security was relaxed. "Here and at most other places we were allowed to go where we pleased, no guard being with us on the route."

The Atlanta he saw was "a new city, mainly built within a few years."

"Here…new factories of various kinds, mostly for the production of army supplies, were being vigorously undertaken. Most articles were roughly made, but substantial and lasting."

"Montgomery, the first capital of rebeldom, is the only place of note through which we passed in Alabama," he wrote. "The capitol is much like our [Allegheny County] courthouse, and is the only building worth notice in the place…the war has destroyed the business in this city and it looks extremely dull." Copley was referring to the county's second courthouse, which was completed in 1841 and ruined by fire in 1882.

The Confederates' original destination for their prisoners was Mobile, "which we had almost reached, when we were ordered to Richmond." The reason for the change in Confederate plans? General Ulysses S. Grant's attack on Vicksburg endangered Mobile as well.

As a result, the prisoners-of-war train headed back toward Richmond. One stop on the return journey was at Knoxville. Josiah Jr. makes no mention of his brother Albert's capture or wounding and does not mention him being taken off the train. He may not have known anything about the fate of his older sibling.

Union POWs were badly fed all during their journey, often waiting a day or more for rations. "The rebel officers did the best they could for us, but often there were no supplies at hand," Josiah Jr. wrote. "Some of them

Montgomery, Alabama, was the first capital of the Confederacy. When Union prisoner Josiah Copley passed through as a POW in 1863, he thought the capitol building resembled Allegheny County's second courthouse. Image from *Harper's Pictorial History of the Civil War Volume First. Courtesy Senator John Heinz History Center.*

spent their own money freely to supply the want of our men, and Southern soldiers often divided their rations with the prisoners."

While the Northern blockade of Southern ports was having an effect, many Confederates appeared to have embraced the hardships: "The people are the most exaggerated type of the Southern character, yet now making it a matter of pride to dress and live in the plainest and most economical style—the daughters of rich planters dressing in coarse homespun."

In the states south of Virginia, he reported seeing few signs of loyalty to the Union. By 1863, Union supporters who actively opposed secession as partisan fighters had been "hung, or driven from their homes," he wrote. "Where the Unionists took no part in the war, they were not interfered with."

Much of what young Copley saw led him to believe the war would not end quickly. Most Northerners had "no adequate idea of the zealous spirit with which [Southerners] support this rebellion," he wrote in his second story that appeared on February 16. "The female populations of the South particularly excel in a bitter hatred of the North, and they strip their homes of the comforts of life to contribute to the support and efficiency of the soldiers."

The Union blockade of Southern ports and capture of New Orleans had disrupted trade and caused shortages. In response the Confederates

Graveyard at Andersonville Prison. Pittsburgh's Josiah Copley spent his second stint as a POW at that notorious camp. Image from *Harper's Pictorial History of the Civil War Part Second*. *Courtesy Senator John Heinz History Center.*

had begun to set up their own factories, "in a rude and primitive manner, but with an energy that compensates," he wrote. The agricultural richness of the region "makes it idle to expect the South to suffer from the lack of means of subsistence."

"Even should we cut off their communications to the region west of the Mississippi, they could still produce enough of everything, except perhaps wool, to supply the army and people."

Copley also reported evidence of under utilized manpower: "Many who under the conscriptive law are liable to serve, are still at home. In Georgia, I noticed that most of the laborers repairing the railroad were white." He estimated that the South could raise an additional 250,000 troops.

All that said, the Confederacy still faced a major economic problem. "But there is a deep-seated rottenness in their affairs that causes worse forebodings at Richmond than the greatest disaster that has ever befallen their arms," Copley wrote.

Inflation—resulting from the South's "baseless credit system"—was reducing the value of Confederate currency. Southern merchants preferred to be paid in U.S. "greenbacks," valuing them at 160 percent of their face value. Confederate money, on the other hand, was "depreciated at least

75 percent"—$100 might buy just $25 worth of goods. In a few months Confederate bills would "hardly be worth one-tenth their nominal value," Copley predicted.

The Civil War took a very heavy toll on the Copley family. Editor Josiah Copley had begun his career as a newspaperman in Kittanning, Armstrong County, and his biography is included in a 1914 book, *Armstrong County, PA: Her People, Past and Present*.

According to that history, the elder Copley lost two sons in the conflict. John, a soldier with the Ninth Pennsylvania Reserves, was killed in the Battle of South Mountain, Maryland, in September 1862, and Albert died of battle wounds sometime in January 1863. Josiah Jr. rejoined his unit and was captured for the second time at the Battle of Chickamauga in September 1863. This time there was no early release. He was held for seventeen months at several Confederate prisons, including the most notorious one, near Andersonville, Georgia.

PITTSBURGH SHIPS OFFER REFUGE TO ALL UNION WOUNDED

When citizens of Pittsburgh financed two relief ships to care for casualties after the Battle of Shiloh, the doctors and nurses on board "recognized every soldier of the army of the Union as our own."

That policy contrasted to the medical efforts sponsored by other communities. "All the boats which had preceded us specified as the objects of their relief, troops of a particular State," businessman Felix R. Brunot wrote in the *Daily Pittsburgh Gazette* on May 6, 1862. Others "refused to take the sick, their aid being meant only for the wounded." When the steamships *Marango* and *J.W. Hallman* arrived, appropriately enough, at Pittsburgh Landing, Tennessee, on April 16, the healthcare staff began to care for everyone. Every soldier, "whether sick or wounded, [was] entitled to our gratitude and such aid as we could give," Brunot wrote.

Born in 1820 and trained as a civil engineer, Brunot earned his fortune in grain milling and steel making. During the Civil War, he turned his attentions to the relief of soldiers. Secretary of War Edwin Stanton issued a pass to Brunot that "permitted him to go through the lines at all places to take charge of hospital work," according to writer John Newton Boucher, the author of *A Century and a Half of Pittsburg and Her People*.

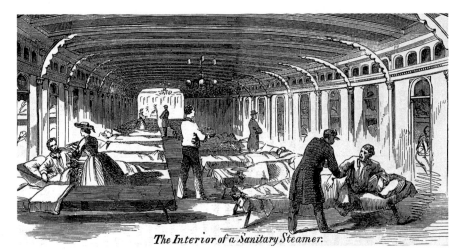

The Interior of a Sanitary Steamer.

The interior of this "sanitary steamer" was similar to that aboard the two steamboats that Pittsburgh sent to aid wounded soldiers after the 1862 Battle of Shiloh. Image from *Harper's Pictorial History of the Civil War Part First. Courtesy Senator John Heinz History Center.*

Army officials ordered the *Marango* to travel about four miles farther downstream on the Tennessee River to pick up sick and wounded soldiers at Crump's Landing. The Pittsburgh team's ship pulled up next to a hospital barge.

"The barge was crowded with men in all stages of diseases—some lying on bunks or cots, many on the floor—with inadequate attendance, no suitable food, almost no medicines and not the slightest approach to the comforts which render sickness tolerable," Brunot wrote. "The atmosphere of the place was so laden with exhalations from the sick as to repel the more timid of our company." Seventy-five of the most seriously ill at Crump's Landing were taken aboard the *Marango*, although "some…seemed already beyond treatment."

"One of the latter, who was rejected because [he appeared] about to die, lay by the passage way. The frequent sight of his youthful and emaciated face excited the sympathy of all, and, at the last moment, he was taken on board," Brunot wrote. The man, thought to be a goner, soon rallied. "He is now fast recovering and in a few days will be with his mother," Brunot wrote. "But few of these men would have lived, but for the effort you have made for their relief," he wrote in his newspaper report to Pittsburgh residents.

The two steamships transported 440 casualties back up the Tennessee and Ohio Rivers, dropping many of the men off at hospitals nearer their homes. Sixty-two soldiers ended up in Allegheny County, most of them admitted to the Marine Hospital in Wood's Run.

Pittsburgh philanthropist Felix Brunot oversaw the care of wounded soldiers at Pittsburg Landing, Tennessee, after the Battle of Shiloh in 1862. He was himself later captured by Confederates. *Courtesy Senator John Heinz History Center.*

Only two months after Brunot returned to Pittsburgh with the Shiloh casualties, he was back in the field. He was overseeing a military hospital near Savage Station, Virginia, when Confederate forces overran it. In its edition on July 9, 1862, the *Pittsburgh Post* had an eyewitness account of Brunot's capture. Robert Kerr, the son of a Pittsburgh lawyer, told the paper "that Mr. Brunot and the nurses were all engaged in ministering to some wounded Union soldiers… when during the fight at that point, the building was entered by a party of rebels, who took prisoners all in the house, except four who escaped." The four who got away included Robert Kerr.

Brunot was freed a few months later in a prisoner exchange, "and for the remainder of the war he was continuously engaged in behalf of the needy soldiers of the northern army," according to Boucher's 1908 book.

REBELS DON "SUNDAY CLOTHING" FOR CHAMBERSBURG RAID

Editors of the *Daily Pittsburgh Gazette* couldn't seem to make up their minds about the accuracy of the latest news from Franklin County. The main headlines on October 14, 1862, "Exciting Rumors!" and "Franklin County Invaded by Thirty Thousand Rebels," were followed by the warning "The Story Probably a Hoax." While there was no mass invasion, it's understandable that journalists were nervous. Chambersburg, the Franklin County seat, had been occupied the previous weekend by 1,800 Confederate cavalrymen commanded by General J.E.B. Stuart.

That same edition of the paper had a story from Frederick, Maryland, describing the success of the secessionists' surprise foray. "The principal object of the rebel raid was to get horses, in which they succeeded, taking back from 800 to 1000 of those, which were seized indiscriminately from the stables of farmers in Pennsylvania. The men also supplied themselves with shoes and clothing from the stores in Chambersburg."

Residents had been taken by surprise when the Confederates arrived on the dark and rainy evening of October 10. Minutes earlier, a messenger rode into town and said he had been chased by Stuart's cavalry through St. Thomas Township, a few miles west of the borough.

"There was an immediate call to arms" but "the rebels were upon us, a detachment having entered under a flag of truce to demand surrender of the place within thirty minutes," according to an October 15 *Gazette* story. About fifty local defenders, known as the "Phil Kearny Infantry," faced the enemy, and their temporary commander, Captain John Eyster, told the Southerners to "Go to h—l!" the story said.

Just before the truce was set to expire, three Chambersburg civilians met with Confederate general Wade Hampton III, one of Stuart's subordinates, and reached terms. "It was agreed that the town should be surrendered on condition that the rights of personal property should be respected," but the secessionists could take "horses, hats, shoes, and such articles as might be useful to them."

"It was a sad spectacle to see rebel soldiers on every

J.E.B. Stuart was a figure to frighten everyone in Pennsylvania in October 1862. Image from *Harper's Pictorial History of the Civil War Part First. Courtesy Senator John Heinz History Center.*

street and street-corner…breaking open and entering the stables of our citizens, and taking out their best horses," the newspaper reported. Railroad equipment and a military warehouse also were destroyed.

The Confederates were otherwise on good behavior: "Gen. Stuart asked one of our citizens if [the Rebels] were as bad as they had been represented, and was told that the devil was never as black as he was painted." One Chambersburg resident was bold enough to ask why the cavalry appeared better dressed than Southern infantry. The horse soldiers "were just now on a visit and had on their Sunday clothing," the cavalryman joked.

Stuart's force arrived on Friday and left around 9:00 a.m. Saturday. They had stayed long enough to provide an opportunity for three Chambersburg residents to reveal Confederate sympathies. Michael Geiselman "furnished the rebels with liquor and regaled them in his house," while Joseph Deckellmayer and William Glenn "congratulated them on their visit." All three were jailed.

"It is in times of invasion that suspected persons should be watched, for then they will likely to expose their treasonable feelings," the newspaper concluded. The raid had succeeded, because "the rebels had sympathizers from our midst giving them information."

The *Gazette*'s first-person account, published initially in the *Chambersburg Dispatch*, concluded with a too-good-to-be-true anecdote featuring a remark "made on the street" by another cheeky foe of the Southerners. As the Confederates rode in, "one of our heroic Union women" protested, "The dirty rebels! to come when they knew we weren't prepared for them!"

"WILDERNESS" BULLET ENDS LIFE OF GENERAL HAYS

After thirty-two battles, Union general Alexander Hays's luck ran out in rural Virginia on May 5, 1864. He was shot in the head and died a few hours later. He became one of the early casualties among the twenty-nine thousand Union and Confederate soldiers killed, wounded or missing during what became known as the Battle of the Wilderness.

A native of Franklin, Venango County, and a graduate of West Point, Hays had served bravely during the Mexican-American War. Resigning his commission, he worked as a railroad construction engineer, iron master and

General Alexander Hays was mortally wounded during the Battle of the Wilderness in 1864. Image from *Harper's Pictorial History of the Civil War Part Second. Courtesy Senator John Heinz History Center.*

miner in the California gold fields. After returning to Pennsylvania, he worked as a civil engineer for the city of Pittsburgh.

When the Civil War broke out, he rejoined the Union army. Serving as colonel of the Sixty-third Pennsylvania Infantry, he took part in much of the early fighting. Leading from the front, he had multiple horses shot out from under him and was wounded twice. His leg was shattered during the Second Battle of Bull Run in August 1862. While "still hobbling on a crutch," he sought to return to service, turning up in Washington, D.C. "His physicians, having examined his wound, declared him totally unfit for duty in the field," according to the November 26, 1862 edition of the *Daily Pittsburgh Gazette*. The story said there was talk in Washington that Hays might be appointed military governor of the national capital, replacing General James S. Wadsworth. That appointment never came through.

Hays eventually got another field command. He led troops at Gettysburg in July 1863 and went south as a brigade commander with General Ulysses S. Grant in the spring of 1864. The Battle of the Wilderness was part of Grant's Overland Campaign, another effort to destroy Robert E. Lee's Army of Northern Virginia.

The battlefield death of Hays on May 5 and funeral on May 14 in Pittsburgh were the subjects of multiple news stories.

His troops had been hammered by a Confederate counterattack led by General James Longstreet. "Gen. Hays with his brigade occupied a front position in the thickest of the fight," the *Gazette* reported on May 16. Riding across his line, he "halted at the head of his old regiment (the 63d)," the story said. "He had scarce paused when a rifle ball struck him just above the cord of his hat, and…he fell insensible to the ground."

Above: Fierce fighting during the three-day Battle of the Wilderness produced almost twenty-nine thousand casualties. Image from *Harper's Pictorial History of the Civil War Part Second. Courtesy Senator John Heinz History Center.*

Left: The body of General Alexander Hays is buried under a monument listing his battles in Allegheny Cemetery. *Courtesy Darrell Sapp of the* Pittsburgh Post-Gazette.

"Thus fell the hero of thirty-two battle fields," the *Gazette* said. "He fell just where he should have wished to have fallen—at the head of his old regiment—the 63d Pennsylvania."

The newspaper story said that Hays was not only valiant himself but also had the power to make others courageous. "His best eulogium is contained in the words of one of his own comrades in arms who said that his simple presence would make a regiment of cowards brave."

On May 14, the day of Hays's funeral, Pittsburgh mayor James Lowry Jr. asked "all manufacturers, shopkeepers and others to close their places of business between the hours of one and five o'clock, that the public may generally have an opportunity to attend the funeral and pay a last tribute to the memory of the illustrious deceased."

Hays's body was moved from the home of his father-in-law, John B. McFaddon, and into the vestibule of First Presbyterian Church, which then faced Wood Street near Sixth Avenue. "Thousands of citizens, of both sexes and of every condition in life, visited the church to look for the last time upon the face of the illustrious patriot," the newspaper said. "Among those who came to gaze on the features of the dead were some who had known him as a soldier and fought under his command."

Reverend William M. Paxton, who gave the eulogy, quoted from a letter Hays had written while a part of Grant's campaign in Virginia. The morning had been beautiful as the troops began their march, Hays wrote, "but it only brought to remembrance, through the throats of many bugles, that duty enjoined upon each one, perhaps before the setting sun, to lay down a life for his country."

Five swords were placed on the general's coffin:

> One—the gift of his early friends and companions in his native town (Franklin), as the reward for his gallantry in the battles of Palo Alto and Resaca de la Palma. Another—a token of affection and admiration from the Texas Rangers. A third—presented to him by his own company (the City Guards)…The fourth—an elegant and expensive sword recently presented to him as a testimony of the confidence and regard of the citizens of Pittsburgh. The fifth—his battle sword, which he carried when he fell on the field of carnage.

Following the service, his funeral cortege moved along Wood Street to Liberty, up Hand Street (now Ninth Street) to what is now Penn Avenue and then out to Allegheny Cemetery in what is now Pittsburgh's Lawrenceville neighborhood. General Hays's body lies there under a granite memorial topped by an eagle and listing the Civil War battles in which he fought.

Chapter 6

The *Gazette* Covers the Capital

WAR WAKES UP WASHINGTON

Previously sleepy Washington has "the press and bustle of New York," a correspondent for the *Daily Pittsburgh Gazette* wrote during his wartime visit to the Federal capital. "Throngs of wagons block up the street, bearing every kind of burden," the reporter wrote on December 21, 1861. New traffic controls were needed, and a "system of policemen at crossings will become a necessity."

The writer of the "Letter from Washington" was identified only by initials: ED. J.A. He apparently was a part-time journalist, as were many nineteenth-century newspaper reporters.

He revealed that the main reason he was visiting Washington was in the hope of getting himself a job in the War Department, then headed by Pennsylvanian Simon Cameron. While waiting several hours for his interview, he caught sight of President Abraham Lincoln and Vice President Hannibal Hamlin, who had come to confer with Cameron. Lincoln looked "so jovial…uttering one or two little jokes," he wrote.

ED. J.A. left Cameron's office disappointed, believing his interview had not been a success: "So the Secretary graciously dismisses you with the promise to keep your documents in view, and you retire, wondering whether you might not as well take your turn at once at the Park Railing."

The railing he referred to was right outside the War Department. He speculated that many other disappointed office-seekers had slammed their

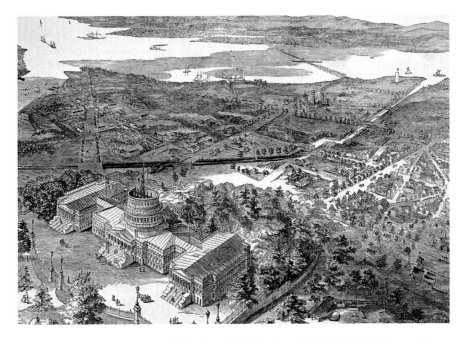

Balloonist's view of Washington during the Civil War shows the half-finished dome of the U.S. Capitol. Image from *Harper's Pictorial History of the Civil War Part First. Courtesy Senator John Heinz History Center.*

hands against it in frustration: "If the iron were more impressionable, it would show him the dents of ten thousand previous fists, all as irate as his own."

Tongue in cheek, he concluded that a man who had failed to get a government job was not feeling "so much grief at his own disappointment, as sorrow in the knowledge that the country cannot last when merit is so neglected."

Pennsylvania, however, had gotten its share of high-level appointments, and the *Gazette* correspondent described three of the most prominent of them.

He took in a review of fifteen thousand volunteer soldiers: "It was a grand sight, and still more pleasant to see the enthusiasm and confidence manifested in our young General and Commander in Chief."

Philadelphia-born general George McClellan was not "the proprietor of a bald head and a shriveled leg," the correspondent wrote. Lincoln, nevertheless, had recognized that the thirty-four-year-old officer, sometimes called the Young Napoleon, linked "brains and judgment to a youth that adds vigor of execution to soundness of conception."

Andrew Carnegie, seen in his office, drew praise for his organizing ability more than thirty years earlier during the first weeks of the Civil War. *Courtesy Senator John Heinz History Center.*

Lincoln had named Thomas Scott, thirty-seven, the general superintendent of the Pennsylvania Railroad, an assistant secretary of war. His task was to oversee military rail transport.

"The National Government has also called from our smoky old burgh, a mere youth in years to take charge of all the national roads and telegraphs," the correspondent wrote. "And the completeness of all the details of work under his charge, has proven how much earnest study and application may

107

secure to the student." The unidentified man the reporter was describing was Scott's young assistant, Andrew Carnegie, age twenty-five.

The *Gazette*'s correspondent also reported on practical aspects of life in wartime Washington. With politicians, soldiers and business people crowding the city, lodgings were scarce.

The reporter agreed to share his small room and bed for a few nights with an unidentified captain on short leave from the 102nd Pennsylvania Regiment, whom he wrote had "the knack of occupying more mattress at one time than any individual I ever had the misfortune to camp with."

A PENNSYLVANIAN FACES RUSSIAN EXILE

Initial rumors going around Washington about the future of Simon Cameron, Abraham Lincoln's ethically challenged secretary of war, soon turned out to be right on the money. "A report is in circulation around the Capitol, and generally believed, that Mr. Cameron has resigned his position as Secretary of War, and that Edwin M. Stanton will take his place," the *Daily Pittsburgh Gazette* reported on January 14, 1862. "Mr. Cameron will be appointed minister to Russia."

At some point that same day, another story confirmed the changes, with the newspaper reporting that Cameron was being sent to St. Petersburg at a time when "our present relations with Europe are deemed highly important [and] the President was anxious that someone should act as Minister…in whom he has entire confidence."

"The capital has just been thrown into a state of intense excitement," the *Gazette* reported the next day. "Speculations are rife as to the cause of this sudden change…no authentic information, however, has been allowed to find its way to the public, notwithstanding the repeated application of anxious inquiries."

In its January 16 edition, the newspaper provided a more cold-eyed explanation of the cabinet moves: Cameron was being politely banished. "A Minister to Russia is only a sort of honorable exile," the *Gazette* said. Cameron was a former Pennsylvania senator who made his fortune in railroads and other businesses. His congressional colleague, Lancaster's Thaddeus Stevens, once had told Lincoln that he didn't think Cameron would steal a red-hot stove. When Cameron took offense, Stevens added to the original insult by offering to take back his remark. Stevens's implication was that his fellow Pennsylvanian just might risk third-degree burns for sufficient financial gain.

Pennsylvania congressman Thaddeus Stevens had little regard for Simon Cameron, Lincoln's first secretary of war. Image of Stevens is from *Harper's Pictorial History of the Civil War Part Second. Courtesy Senator John Heinz History Center.*

Stanton, Cameron's successor, was an Ohio native who had practiced law in Pittsburgh and married a local woman, Ellen Hutchison, who still had family in the city. His selection represented an effort at bipartisanship. He was a Democrat who had supported Lincoln's opponent, Stephen Douglas, during the 1860 election. He also had served as U.S. attorney general during the last months of the foundering administration of James Buchanan. As a Douglas Democrat, he opposed secession and was identified with the antislavery wing of his party.

"The new Secretary of War is called a Pennsylvanian in the New York papers," the *Gazette* reported on January 16. "His strongest trait is an indomitable will, which is coupled with untiring energy…we trust he may direct all his great energies to the early overthrow of the rebellion."

The *Pittsburgh Post* editor James P. Barr was delighted with Lincoln's pick. He had no use for Cameron. When some newspapers speculated that Cameron might have been sacked because of his support of quick emancipation and arming of slaves, Barr was incredulous. "It has been very well established in the last ten years that he has no political principles," Barr wrote of Cameron on January 16. "He has boxed the compass, belonging to every political organization in the country, not in pursuit of principle, but of office."

The *Gazette* was more generous in its analysis. "Numerous frauds had come to light in the [War Department's] contracting department, which needed ventilating and exposing, and a new man could probably perform this work better than Mr. Cameron, who has doubtless been imposed upon by friends he had trusted," the newspaper concluded on January 20.

EMANCIPATION ARRIVES EARLY

April 16 is remembered as Emancipation Day every year in Washington, D.C. It has nothing to do with the IRS tax deadline a day earlier. The holiday marks the day in 1862 when slaves in the nation's capital were freed.

"The hearts of all the friends of freedom are rejoiced by the report just made current that Mr. Lincoln has signed the bill for the emancipation of the blacks of this District," the *Daily Pittsburgh Gazette* reported on April 18, 1862. The law passed by Congress called for slave owners to be paid $300 for each person granted freedom. The measure predated the Emancipation Proclamation, which freed all slaves in the rebelling Confederate states, by more than eight months.

While the *Gazette* praised Congress and Abraham Lincoln, the *Pittsburgh Post* was scornful of the president and the new law. Lincoln had dithered for several days before signing the measure, the *Post* said in its April 18 edition. That delay gave slaveholders a chance to transport their more valuable "property" to neighboring Maryland, a border state where the emancipation law would not apply. The newspaper concluded that "the late emancipation act is a total failure…it merely throws upon their own resources a class of people, old and young, who are totally incapable of turning to any advantage the sudden liberty which has been given them." *Post* editor James P. Barr called the measure "an act of cruelty to the slaves."

The *Post*'s alternative was "gradual emancipation," the policy that had been adopted by Pennsylvania in 1780. The policy provided that those

Lincoln's decision to free the slaves—first in Washington and then throughout the Confederacy—drew scorn from many, including Southern artist Adalbert Volck. His drawing shows Lincoln with his foot on the U.S. Constitution and dipping his pen into a devil's inkwell. *Courtesy the* Pittsburgh Post-Gazette.

currently enslaved were to remain slaves, but the future children of slaves would be freed. But that event would occur only after the offspring had worked long enough to compensate their parents' owners for the costs of providing food, clothing and shelter. In return, owners would be compelled to "provide for the old, worn-out bondsmen."

The *Gazette* mocked the proposal. The Democrats had decades to push that agenda, but "never by act or word showed the disposition to inaugurate" such a policy, the newspaper said the next day. Two weeks later, the *Gazette*'s Washington correspondent reported on how the District's African

Americans reacted to the emancipation law during a May 1 "day of solemn thanksgiving to God."

"So the joy over their deliverance here found expressions in assembling in their churches, in prayer, in singing," the anonymous journalist wrote in a story that appeared on May 6. As many as 1,500 people, all but a dozen of them black, gathered near the Capitol building in Asbury Chapel to hear speeches and sing hymns. "Did anyone ever hear sweeter voices than were there?" the reporter asked. "I never did."

"Several colored men addressed their people in remarks characterized by practical good sense and abounding with wholesome advice," he wrote. When a collection was taken up to help support escaped slaves—"the poor refugees who daily reach this city from the blasted wastes of Virginia"—$100 was raised in less than ten minutes. That number is equal to more than $2,300 in modern currency.

The reporter was impressed that people who had very little were generous to those who had even less. The relief funds were raised among people who "were but last week…chattels, things to be 'whipped on the bare back,' to have 'their ears clipped,' to be fined $5 for holding religious or other meetings without permission, later than 10 p.m."

PITTSBURGHER'S VISIT TO JEFF DAVIS PROVES A HOAX

Michaele and Tareq Salahi, the Virginia couple who talked their way into a 2009 State Dinner hosted by Barack and Michelle Obama, would have had a much easier time getting into the White House when Abraham Lincoln lived there. As illustrated in the Steven Spielberg movie about the sixteenth president, Lincoln devoted some of his office hours to a "public opinion bath" where visitors could petition or just visit with him.

On November 19, 1862, Lincoln met at the White House with J. Wesley Greene, who described himself as a Pittsburgh businessman, to hear about two conversations the man claimed to have had in Richmond with Confederate president Jefferson Davis. Greene said he "had done Mr. Davis some service during the Mexican war, which he (Davis) gratefully remembered," according to a story that appeared on December 11, 1862, in the *New York Times*. An unlikely choice as a messenger, Greene claimed that he had been selected as a go-between "because he was unknown to fame as a politician."

Greene worked as a journeyman japanner in a Pittsburgh metalware shop at the corner of Market Street and what is now the Boulevard of the Allies, according to a December 13 story in the *Daily Pittsburgh Gazette*. (A japanner was a craftsman who applied hard, black varnish onto decorative metal objects.)

Greene's first-person account, which the New York newspaper quoted, had been published on December 10 in the *Chicago Times*. According to that story, Davis told Greene that he "desired a termination of the war, and an amicable adjustment of the difficulties between the North and the South." Among his proposed terms for an end to the Civil War, Davis purportedly wanted amnesty for himself and "all political offenders," the "restoration of all fugitive slaves" to their owners and the withdrawal of Lincoln's Emancipation Proclamation, scheduled to take effect January 1, 1863.

"Mr. Lincoln's Proclamation to liberate the slaves seemed to annoy Mr. Davis, who casually remarked, that 'It would play hell with us,'" Greene wrote. "Mr. Davis said that the proclamation of Mr. Lincoln was regarded throughout the South as a bid for a 'servile insurrection.'"

The White House confirmed that Lincoln had met once with Greene, but the president wasn't buying his tale after deciding "the entire story was a very shallow attempt at deception," the New York newspaper reported. Greene was called "The Greatest Humbug of the Day" in a December 13 headline in the *Daily Pittsburgh Gazette*, which had investigated his background. He had arrived in Pittsburgh in the summer of 1861. He presented letters of reference from ministers in Buffalo and Cincinnati to the pastor of the city's First Methodist Church attesting to his suitability as a preacher. Those letters turned out to be forgeries, the newspaper wrote. The Methodists' investigation also found that Greene had left behind several ex-wives and children. He was "read out of the church" but otherwise "permitted to go his way."

A letter from Greene's employer, John Dunlap, punched the biggest hole in his mission-to-Richmond story. Dunlap wrote that he had been at work in Pittsburgh on the dates when he claimed to have been meeting with Davis. Greene disappeared from the city before the *Gazette*'s December 13 story appeared. The woman believed to be his fourth wife had left days earlier, telling friends she was going back east. The newspaper concluded, however, that she and her husband probably had taken refuge in a place few Pittsburghers would ever willingly reside: Cleveland.

Chapter 7

As the Guns Fall Silent

PITTSBURGH MOURNS LINCOLN'S DEATH

Abraham Lincoln was shot by an assassin on Good Friday 1865 and died early on Holy Saturday. The next day, Easter Sunday, Allegheny County residents filled churches as their pastors sought to provide some comfort and understanding following the first murder of a United States president.

Lincoln was born poor and arrived at middle age "unknown, save to a limited circle of political friends," the Reverend E.B. Snyder said in his sermon that Sunday at Christ Methodist Episcopal Church. His church was on what is now Pittsburgh's North Side. "So little was Mr. Lincoln known to fame, so untried and inexperienced was he in civil affairs…that many of the best and wisest men of the land felt that committing the reins of the government into his hands was, at best, but an experiment," he said.

"But Mr. Lincoln was a child of Providence," the pastor told his flock, according to a *Daily Pittsburgh Gazette* story that appeared on April 17, 1865. "God saw that he was the right man for the right place at the right time." While men die, the nation lives. "As in the church, God takes away the workman but the work goes on," Reverend Snyder said.

Thanks to the telegraph, news of the president's shooting had reached Pittsburgh shortly after the unnamed assassin's attack. The *Gazette* on Saturday, April 15, had a fairly complete first-day, front-page story about both the fatal attack on Lincoln and the stabbing of William Seward, the

DEATH OF ABRAHAM LINCOLN.
April 15 1865.

Above: The death of Abraham Lincoln generated an outpouring of grief across the North. *Courtesy Senator John Heinz History Center.*

Left: Secretary of State William Seward was attacked and almost killed the same night as Abraham Lincoln was shot. Image from *Harper's Pictorial History of the Civil War Part First. Courtesy Senator John Heinz History Center.*

secretary of state, at his home. Journalism is a rough draft of history, and the biggest error that morning was an all-capital-letters subhead in the *Gazette* that predicted "THE SECRETARY WILL PROBABLY DIE."

Lincoln died early Saturday. By Monday, John Wilkes Booth, a well-known actor, had been identified as the assassin (though his last name was being spelled Boothe). The suspect's brother, the more famous Edwin Booth, was not a suspect. Edwin Booth "has been throughout a Union man," the *Gazette* reported that day. "He has played on different occasions [in New York City] for the benefit of the Sanitary Commission, and in many other ways has shown his sympathy with the Union cause."

That day's paper also contained the news that "SEWARD WILL RECOVER" and an erroneous report picked up from the *New York Herald*: "Boothe has been arrested near Baltimore, and will be placed for safekeeping on board a monitor at the Navy Yard" in Washington. ("Monitor" was both the name of the navy's first ironclad warship and the name given to a class of small, heavily armed naval vessels.)

As the nation went into mourning, public events were called off. A classified notice in the *Gazette* alerted residents that "the First Annual Ball of the Niagara Steam Fire Engine and Hose Company, which was to have taken place at Concert Hall this evening, has been postponed until further notice in consequence of the death of President Lincoln."

The next day's paper included a report on an outdoor meeting held Monday, April 17, outside the post office, at what is now Fifth Avenue and Smithfield Street. That session was to decide on how the city should mark the president's death. The story described "spontaneous abandonment of the people of all their ordinary avocations and the closing of their places of business from Saturday morning until Monday night." Those actions "indicate the universal regard and respect for the lamentable dead, and the deep gloom which pervades all hearts on account of the great national loss we deplore."

Black crepe hanging on public buildings should remain for a month and any symbols of mourning on private homes should stay up until Lincoln's funeral, according to the report. "Citizens generally [are] requested to wear an appropriate badge of mourning for thirty days," the story advised.

Lincoln had passed through Allegheny City and Pittsburgh in February 1861 on the way to his inauguration in Washington. The initial expectation was that the funeral train carrying his body back to Springfield, Illinois, would retrace that route in reverse, making stops in Pittsburgh, Harrisburg and Philadelphia. Whenever Lincoln's body arrived here, Mayor James Lowry

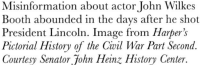

Misinformation about actor John Wilkes Booth abounded in the days after he shot President Lincoln. Image from *Harper's Pictorial History of the Civil War Part Second*. *Courtesy Senator John Heinz History Center.*

and a special committee were to "take the necessary measures for a general funeral escort by our entire population and for such other ceremonies as in their judgement may be appropriate to the said occasion."

That final goodbye was not to be. When Secretary of War Edwin Stanton arranged the itinerary for Lincoln's funeral train, he dropped both Pittsburgh and Cincinnati from the route in favor of a new stop in Chicago.

ANDREW JOHNSON FACES A TOUGH CROWD

President Andrew Johnson wasn't feeling the love when he arrived in Steubenville, Ohio, on September 13, 1866. His reception there should have given him a hint of what he had to look forward to when he arrived later that day in Pittsburgh.

Johnson was a Tennessee Democrat who joined Abraham Lincoln as his vice-presidential running mate on a National Union Party ticket during the dark days of the Civil War. He became president upon the death of Lincoln, but he had quickly run into a buzz saw of Republican criticism that he was

President Andrew Johnson was booed during his 1866 visit to Pittsburgh. Image from *Harper's Pictorial History of the Civil War Part Second. Courtesy Senator John Heinz History Center.*

too forgiving of the recently rebellious South.

Just before the midterm congressional elections, he undertook a whistle-stop campaign to build support for his policies. He arranged to be accompanied by several Civil War heroes, including General Ulysses S. Grant, Admiral David Farragut and General George Custer.

When Custer introduced Johnson in Steubenville as "the chief magistrate of the nation," the president stepped forward and bowed. "While Mr. Johnson was bowing there was a perfect stillness, but when he attempted to speak there was some confusion in the crowd," a reporter for the *Daily Pittsburgh Gazette* wrote the next day. "[I]mmediately after there were loud cheers for the president, intermingled with hisses, groans and cries of 'Grant, Grant.'" Things were to get much worse in Pittsburgh.

After the presidential party arrived at Union Depot, which was very near the site of the modern Amtrak Station in downtown Pittsburgh, Johnson and the other visitors transferred to carriages for a procession through crowded city streets. It became clear that most people had not turned out to see the president. "The carriage containing Mr. Johnson was frequently permitted to pass almost unnoticed…while the carriage in which Grant and Farragut rode was greeted with the wildest enthusiasm."

The parade ended on Wood Street at the St. Charles Hotel, now the site of Point Park University's Lawrence Hall. The first lines of Johnson's speech there were greeted by cheers, according to the newspaper, but as he made his case for easing the return of the Southern states into the Union, many in the crowd grew hostile. "What about Jeff Davis?" someone in the crowd yelled.

"The friends of President Johnson on the platform with him urged him to go on and not mind the interruption, but the confusion was so tremendous that it was impossible," the *Gazette* reported. For the next ten minutes, "Every imaginable cry resounded on every side." Johnson tried several times to continue, but the noise from the crowd did not abate.

Another fifteen minutes passed, and "the whole space about the hotel was a moving sea of men and boys, each individual in it crying out at the top of his voice. Calls for Grant became louder and more frequent, until at last no other word could be heard." Grant, who was a serving military officer, was in a sensitive position, because Johnson was his commander in chief. Finally, he came forward, bowed and waved to the crowd, but he said nothing. Johnson then gave up and left the platform, "followed by cries and groans, mingled with a few cheers."

His reception in Pittsburgh was a sign of worse things to come. In 1868, the House of Representatives impeached him, but GOP leaders in the Senate could not muster the necessary two-thirds majority needed to remove him from office. Denied renomination by the Democrats, Johnson was followed as president in 1869 by, not surprisingly, General Grant.

GRAND ARMY OF THE REPUBLIC VETERANS MARCH IN FINAL MUSTER

Jacob Mooker sought no special treatment because of his age. The ninety-seven-year-old Union army veteran marched from Pittsburgh's North Side through downtown, past a reviewing stand on Grant Street.

He was among 140 "Boys in Blue" who attended the Grand Army of the Republic's (GAR) 1939 National Encampment in Pittsburgh. He was the only member of the veterans' contingent to walk the two-mile length of the parade route. "If I can't walk the full way, what's the point of me marching at all," he told a reporter for the *Pittsburgh Post-Gazette* in a story that appeared on August 31.

The rest of the marchers—average age ninety-five—rode in open cars along most of the route. About forty cane-carrying veterans, however, got out of their vehicles and walked past the reviewing stand. "The tap, tap, tap of the canes on the pavement could be heard even above the applause of the spectators," writer Gilbert Love wrote in that same day's edition of the *Pittsburgh Press*.

Marlin J. Warner, a spry ninety-four-year-old of Grand Rapids, Michigan, danced with Mrs. T.S. Rufenact, the daughter of one of his Civil War comrades, during the 1939 GAR Encampment in Pittsburgh. *Courtesy the* Pittsburgh Post-Gazette.

Like his former comrades, Mooker, a resident of Valparaiso, Indiana, made a slight concession to his advanced years. He used a walking stick, fashioned from the trunk of a discarded Christmas tree and decorated with red, white and blue streamers, Love wrote.

The Grand Army of the Republic, an organization of men who had served in Union forces during the Civil War, had almost 500,000 members at its peak. By the time of its seventy-third meeting in Pittsburgh, its rolls were down to 1,700 old soldiers.

Members had a busy agenda during the six-day event. In addition to participating in the parade, about one hundred attended the opening of the Allegheny County Fair at South Park. The veterans told stories and sang songs during a program at Soldiers & Sailors Memorial Hall in Oakland. At their business meetings, they passed resolutions protesting the soon-to-be-released film version of *Gone with the Wind*.

GAR members voted to "absent themselves" from any theater showing the "defamatory film," which was based on Margaret Mitchell's bestselling novel. They specifically objected to the film's presentation of General William T. Sherman's march across Georgia and the portrayal of a Union soldier as a "hideous marauder, attacking women," according to a September 1 story in the *Post-Gazette*.

They also opposed other measures to "palliate the treason of the South." Those included a congressional bill to provide $25,000 for a statue of Stonewall Jackson and an offer from the United Daughters of the Confederacy to present a Robert E. Lee Memorial Sword to a West Point cadet each year.

Mrs. Walter D. Lamar, president-general of the Confederate Daughters, warned that the GAR's actions "may cripple the fine relations between the Grand Army of the Republic and the Confederate Veterans."

Gone with the Wind was still in the final stages of production when the GAR took its stand, and neither its supporters nor detractors had yet seen the film. It would have its premiere in December 1939.

As they wrapped up their encampment, the Civil War veterans shared space in Pittsburgh newspapers with another conflict. "Polish Cities Bombed" was the *Post-Gazette*'s banner headline on September 1. World War II had begun with the German invasion of Poland.

GAR POSTSCRIPT

When Joseph Caldwell died on August 30, 1946, he was the last surviving member of the last Pittsburgh-area post of the Grand Army of the Republic. He was ninety-eight.

Born in Allegheny City on November 13, 1847, Caldwell was sixteen when he enlisted as a private in the third version of Captain Joseph M. Knap's independent artillery battery. Caldwell's was a hundred-day emergency enlistment, and he served from May 19 until September 15, 1864, according to Michael Kraus, curator at Soldiers & Sailors Memorial Hall and Museum in Oakland.

The GAR was organized first into local posts and then into state or regional departments. Because membership was limited to Civil War service members, posts lasted only until their last member-veteran died. He was the last member of McPherson Post 117.

When Joseph Caldwell died in 1946, he was the last member of the last GAR post in the Pittsburgh area. *Courtesy the* Pittsburgh Post-Gazette.

Caldwell's obituary in the August 31 edition of the *Pittsburgh Post-Gazette* said that he had attended every local Memorial Day parade for eighty years. Blind, almost deaf and suffering from a heart ailment, he had been unable to attend the 1946 Memorial Day commemoration, so "the South Hills Memorial Association went to him. Major General Manton S. Eddy…made a brief speech at his bedside."

After the war, he had worked as a contractor in Allegheny and Butler Counties, retiring about 1926. He lived in Pittsburgh's Brookline neighborhood for most of that time but was residing with his son, Paul, in Overbrook when he died. He was buried in Summit United Presbyterian Cemetery in Jefferson, Butler County. The graveyard was not far from a farm he owned in Butler Township.

Caldwell was the last man surviving out of a total of 25,930 residents of Allegheny County who served with Union forces during the Civil War. About 3,000—more than 10 percent—were killed or wounded during the conflict, according to Soldiers & Sailors records.

Bibliography and Further Reading

Baldwin, Leland D. *Pittsburgh: The Story of a City*. Pittsburgh, PA: University of Pittsburgh Press, 1970.

Barcousky, Len. *Remembering Pittsburgh: An "Eyewitness" History of the Steel City*. Charleston, SC: The History Press, 2010.

Beers, J.H., and Company. *Armstrong County, Pennsylvania: Her People Past and Present*. Chicago, IL: J.H. Beers and Company, 1914.

Donald, David Herbert. *Lincoln*. New York: Touchstone, 1995.

Fox, Arthur B. *Our Honored Dead: Allegheny County, Pennsylvania in the American Civil War*. Chicora, PA: Mechling Bookbindery, 2008.

———. *Pittsburgh During the American Civil War: 1860–1865*. Chicora, PA: Mechling Bookbindery, 2002.

Guernsey, Alfred H., and Henry M. Alden. *Harper's Pictorial History of the Civil War, Part First*. Chicago: McDonald Bros., 1866.

———. *Harper's Pictorial History of the Civil War, Part Second*. Chicago: McDonald Bros., 1868.

Thomas, Clarke M. *Front-Page Pittsburgh: Two Hundred Years of the* Post-Gazette. Pittsburgh, PA: University of Pittsburgh Press, 2005.

Index

A

Alexander, Mayor Alexander C. 69
Allegheny Arsenal 9
Allegheny Cemetery 61, 86, 104
Anderson, Major Robert 25, 33, 34
Andersonville Prison 97
Antietam, Battle of 59, 62, 88

B

Baldwin, Leland D. 77
Barr, James P. 19, 64, 67, 77, 110
Batchelor, Capt. C.W. 48
Batchelor, Stanton 48
Beckham, Lee A. 55
Bell, John 23
Black, Col. Samuel 41
Booth, John Wilkes 33, 116
Boucher, John Newton 97
Brady, Capt. E.R. 64
Breckenridge, John 23
Brooks, Gen. William T.H. 71
Brown, Thornsbury Bailey 40
Brunot, Felix R. 97
Buchanan, James 24, 32, 109
Bull Run, First Battle of 82
Bull Run, Second Battle of 87, 102
Burnside, Gen. Ambrose 90
Butler, Gen. Benjamin 82

C

Caldwell, Joseph 121
Cameron, Simon 41, 105, 108
Campbell, Capt. David 37
Camp Curtin 41
Camp Tennally 42
Carnegie, Andrew 108
Chambersburg, 1862 Confederate raid
    of 99
Collins, Mary "May" 62
Connellsville 40
Copley, Albert 93, 97
Copley, John 87, 97
Copley, Josiah, Jr. 11, 93
Copley, Josiah, Sr. 87, 94, 97
Curtin, Gov. Andrew 22, 37, 41, 53, 75
Custer, Gen. George 118

D

Davidson, Col. Daniel R. 40
Davis, Jefferson 15, 32, 53, 67, 112

Douglas, Stephen 23, 109
Dunlap, John 113
Duquesne Greys 37

E

Eberhart, Conrad 58
Emancipation Day 110
Emancipation Proclamation 62, 65, 71, 110, 113
Errett, Russell 25, 53, 63
Eyster, Capt. John 100

F

Farragut, Admiral David 118
Faulkner, William 9
Floyd, John B. 25, 32, 47
Fort Donelson, capture of 47
Fort Pitt Foundry 37, 70
Fortress Monroe 82
Fort Sumter 20, 33, 34
Fox, Arthur B. 38
Fredericksburg, Battle of 90
Frick, J.R. 61
Fyffe, Col. Edward P. 56

G

Garfield, James A. 49
Gettysburg, Battle of 72, 102
Graham, James 81
Grand Army of the Republic 119, 121
Grant, Ulysses S. 47, 50, 94, 102, 118
Gray, Marie 62
Grinnell, David 31
Guiteau, Charles 50

H

Hamlin, Ellen 45
Hamlin, Hannibal 43, 105
Hays, Gen. Alexander 101
Heinrichs, J.E. 58
Homewood Cemetery 31
Hooker, Gen. Joseph 88
Horne, Joseph 72

Hutchison, Ellen 30, 109
Hutchison, James Adam, Jr. 30

J

Johnson, Andrew 45, 79, 117
Jones and Laughlin 71

K

Kelly, Megyn 77
Knap's independent artillery battery 121

L

Lee, Robert E. 11, 69, 88, 89, 91, 102
Libby Prison 94
Lincoln, Abraham 11, 12, 15, 22, 23, 24, 27, 43, 45, 53, 62, 65, 69, 74, 79, 105, 110, 112, 114
Lincoln, Mary Todd 43, 47
Longstreet, Gen. James 102
Lowry, Mayor James 104, 116

M

Manassas, Second Battle of 55
McClellan, George 55, 79, 85, 89, 106
McNash, Henry, tobacco chewer 68
Monongahela House 17, 71
Mooker, Jacob 119
Moorhead, James K. 27, 84
Moorhead, Mary 84

N

Negley, James S. 19, 85
Nicholson, Alfred Osborn Pope 85
Ninth Pennsylvania Reserve Corps 42

O

Obama, Barack 77
102nd Pennsylvania Regiment 108
Owston, Capt. Charles William 86

P

Pittsburgh Rifles 86, 88
Pittsburgh Sanitary Fair 74

R

roast cat, lawsuit over 58

S

Sahl, Capt. Leopold, Jr. 51
Sahl, Col. Leopold 52
Scheib, Robert J., Sr. 62
Senator John Heinz History Center 9,
        17, 30
Seventy-eighth Pennsylvania Infantry 93
Seventy-seventh Pennsylvania
        Volunteer Infantry 57
Seward, William 114
Shannon, Judge Peter 37
Shields, James 45
Shiloh, Battle of 50, 56, 97
Sixty-second Pennsylvania Volunteers 41
Sixty-third Pennsylvania Infantry
        Regiment 102
South Mountain, Battle of 86, 97
Stanton, Edwin M. 27, 30, 108
Stevens, Thaddeus 108
St. Mary's Cemetery 52
Stuart, J.E.B. 11, 69, 99

T

Teutonia Maennerchor 77

U

United States Colored Troops 65

W

Walker, Susan Cooper 17
Wells, Terry H. 31
Western Pennsylvania Hospital 77
Wide Awakes marching society 21
Wilderness, Battle of 101
Wilkins, Judge William 37

Wilson, Daisy Davis 19
Wilson, Mayor George 19, 26

About the Author

A veteran journalist, Len Barcousky has worked for newspapers in New York and Pennsylvania. He is a graduate of Penn State, where he earned a bachelor's degree with high honors in English, and of Columbia University, where he received a master of business administration degree. Since 1986, he has been an editor and reporter at the *Pittsburgh Post-Gazette*, the oldest newspaper west of the Allegheny Mountains. He and his wife, Barbara, live in Ben Avon, Pennsylvania.